100 Roses for the South Florida Garden

UNIVERSITY PRESS OF FLORIDA

Florida A&M University, Tallahassee
Florida Atlantic University, Boca Raton
Florida Gulf Coast University, Ft. Myers
Florida International University, Miami
Florida State University, Tallahassee
New College of Florida, Sarasota
University of Central Florida, Orlando
University of Florida, Gainesville
University of North Florida, Jacksonville
University of South Florida, Tampa
University of West Florida, Pensacola

100 ROSES
for the South
Florida Garden

Victor Lazzari

UNIVERSITY PRESS OF FLORIDA

Gainesville · Tallahassee · Tampa · Boca Raton
Pensacola · Orlando · Miami · Jacksonville · Ft. Myers · Sarasota

Frontispiece: 'Granada' (hybrid tea rose), introduced in 1963.

28 27 26 25 24 23   6 5 4 3 2 1

Library of Congress Cataloging-in-Publication Data
Names: Lazzari, Victor, author.
Title: 100 roses for the South Florida garden / Victor Lazzari.
Other titles: One hundred roses for the South Florida garden
Description: 1. | Gainesville : University Press of Florida, 2023. |
Includes bibliographical references and index.
Identifiers: LCCN 2022043294 (print) | LCCN 2022043295 (ebook) | ISBN
9780813068879 (paperback) | ISBN 9780813072647 (ebook)
Subjects: LCSH: Roses—Florida. | Gardening—Florida. | Rose
culture—Florida. | BISAC: GARDENING / Flowers / Roses | GARDENING /
Climatic / Tropical
Classification: LCC SB411 .L37 2023 (print) | LCC SB411 (ebook) | DDC
635.9/3364409759—dc23/eng/20220928
LC record available at https://lccn.loc.gov/2022043294
LC ebook record available at https://lccn.loc.gov/2022043295

The University Press of Florida is the scholarly publishing agency for the State University
System of Florida, comprising Florida A&M University, Florida Atlantic University, Florida
Gulf Coast University, Florida International University, Florida State University, New College
of Florida, University of Central Florida, University of Florida, University of North Florida,
University of South Florida, and University of West Florida.

University Press of Florida
2046 NE Waldo Road
Suite 2100
Gainesville, FL 32609
http://upress.ufl.edu

This book is dedicated to my partner, Brian Michael Bocci.
How a self-professed neat freak could fall in love with the world's messiest
gardener is a miracle for which I am eternally grateful—
thank you always and forever, Brian.

Contents

'Smokin' Hot', a hybrid tea, displays smoldering blooms against the dramatic architecture of the Vizcaya rose garden in Miami.

1

By Any Other Name

Picture it: the Maryland suburbs circa 1988. Reagan is in the White House, Madonna and Prince are on the radio, and my seven-year-old self is sequestered in the fenced-in backyard of the family townhouse. It is late May, under sunny skies. There's a tidy tangle of Mid-Atlantic garden fare: Junipers, spireas, the rotting leaves of April's tulips and daffodils. An Eastern white pine sits in one corner of the back yard; my mother's vegetable plot fills the other.

That's when I see it.

Sprawling up the pine tree and over the fence is some sort of vining plant covered in huge yellow flowers. Upon closer inspection, this is no vine; it's more like a climbing shrub, with thick, thorny stems. We were learning about the Middle Ages in elementary school, and this plant's prickly canes give me the impression of an armored knight—a hero, but also a warrior. Despite the thorns, my scrawny arm reaches up to the nearest flower anyway. Snaps it off. It's huge, shaped like a cup, and looks like it was made for smelling. I go in for the sniff and . . . *ohhhhhhh.*

When asked about my earliest memory of roses, I always circle back to finding 'Royal Gold', a fairly common yellow climbing rose in the 1980s, dominating the fence of my childhood home. My parents were "weekend gardeners"—clip the hollies, plant a few tomato seedlings—but neither of them had much interest in roses when I was a child, and the 'Royal Gold' specimen was most likely planted by our home's previous owner.

In some ways, the green leftovers from past tenants are the best forays into gardening, especially for small children. Adult gardeners take great pride in "firsts"—the first new tree or new flowerbed that they install in their home—

but children remember, with startling clarity, the *old stuff*. The old lilac from which they gathered bouquets every spring or the old crabapple tree that served as both second base *and* unlimited ammunition supplies.

Such was my childhood experience with 'Royal Gold'. Suddenly finding this massive, bulky plant laden with delicate, sweetly fragrant flowers—a living yin/yang, though I was too young to grasp this concept—made me feel like I had just made a new friend.

My interest in roses grew from there. When we moved into a large, tacky colonial knockoff in the early 1990s, I immediately asked permission to plant roses around the quarter-acre yard. Happy to be relieved of extra yard work, my dad eagerly agreed; by the time I entered high school, I had about 30 varieties. I began dutifully studying how to take care of my new green friends: soil prep, fertilizing, watering, pruning.

But, best of all, I learned the incredible story of the rose.

ROSE HISTORY

The story of the rose stretches back about 4,000 years. Two epicenters of rose domestication seem to have occurred almost simultaneously: archaeological evidence shows that both the ancient Sumerians and the ancient Chinese each cultivated the wild roses in their lands beginning around 2,000 BCE.

It's crucial to note that these two cultures were separated by thousands of miles, with no known contact with each other at that time. Furthermore, the wild roses in their ancient lands looked nothing like the chiseled flowers that adorn our modern-day weddings, funerals, graduations, beauty pageants, and "I'm sorry, honey" bouquets. The implication is clear: even in her most primitive form, the rose had the ability to charm and seduce humans of all sorts.

The ancient Egyptians probably learned of roses through their close proximity and various exchanges (including wars) with the Sumerians. As roses became popular in ancient Egypt, other nearby cultures soon caught on: the Babylonians, Greeks, and Romans all eagerly grew the flowers, documented their cultivation, used them for everything from decorations to medicines, and enshrined their beauty in murals, pottery, songs, and poems. Most famously, in 600 BCE, the Greek poet Sappho gave the rose its everlasting title: "the Queen of all flowers."

Around the same time that Sappho bestowed her crown upon the rose, the

'Cyd's Compassion' displays charming, old-fashioned flowers in heavy flushes all year long in South Florida.

Chinese scholar Confucius observed that both the Imperial Gardens *and* the Imperial Library of the Zhou Emperor were full of roses: plants in one; books and scrolls in the other. Meanwhile, in ancient India, the Hindus claimed that two of their most important gods—Brahma the Creator and Vishnu the Preserver—were having a heated debate about which flower was the most beautiful. Brahma favored the lotus blossom while Vishnu favored the rose. According to legend, Vishnu then showed Brahma an arbor overflowing with climbing roses in his garden, and Brahma finally conceded the rose's superior beauty.

Roses reached their first zenith in ancient Rome, where they became a financially lucrative crop for the empire. The flower was a staple of Roman life, used for everything from signifying private meetings ("sub rosa," literally "under the rose") to decorating orgies. After the fall of Rome in 395 CE, rose cultivation continued on in the adjacent Persian Empire; to this day, roses are

Roses and herbs make wonderful organic garden playmates. Here, the fragrant 'Richard's Rose' is set off with drifts of culinary rosemary.

still a major cultural cornerstone of the modern countries that occupy Persia's former territory.

In northern Europe, medieval monks kept roses in their monasteries and cloister gardens, and the rose transformed from a symbol of Roman decadence into one of Christian martyrdom. The symbolism of the rose culminated in England's infamous War of the Roses in 1455, where the Houses of York and Lancaster (represented by a white and a red rose, respectively) fought for claim to the English throne.

But it wasn't until 1804 that roses reached their second zenith. That was when Empress Josephine of France, wife of Napoleon, let her personal obsession with roses metastasize into a project unprecedented in human history: collecting every variety of rose in existence and building the world's most extravagant rose garden at the royal palace of Chateau Malmaison.

We don't know if Josephine realized the extent to which the Malmaison project would change roses drastically and permanently, but that's exactly what happened. Josephine didn't just seize all the different roses available in Europe; she used her husband's far-reaching political power to request roses from all over the known world, especially East Asia. Four Chinese roses in particular—we now call them the "Four Stud Chinas"—made their way into France and led to such changes in the flower that entirely new classes of roses emerged as a result.

The Malmaison garden also led to the massive separation of all rose classes into two broad categories: modern roses—those created after 1867—and the somewhat-ageist "old" roses, all the ones that existed prior to then.

ROSE CLASSES—OLD ROSES

The Euro-Mediterranean Roses

There are five main classes of Euro-Mediterranean roses, unified by large, voluptuously petaled flowers, heady fragrances, and a preference for cold-winter climates.

GALLICAS. *Rosa gallica*, the gallica rose or French rose, is native throughout Western Europe. It blooms for about a month in late spring with semidouble, deep pink flowers. This species is also called the apothecary's rose due to its long history in European medicine as a remedy for countless ailments.

The gallica class, which includes selections and hybrids of this species, comprises relatively short (5' or less) shrubs, with a dense, upright habit. Flowers are usually deep shades of pink, maroon, and purplish red and tend to be strongly fragrant, including a unique myrrh scent that has played prominently in the programs of contemporary breeders.

Gallicas need an annual period of winter chill to set flower buds; for that reason, they perform poorly in South Florida.

DAMASKS. The original damask rose, *Rosa × damascena*, was named for the ancient city of Damascus, where it was first encountered almost 3,000 years ago. Damask roses bloom in shades of pink and white and are blessed with an overpowering tangy-sweet perfume that is now permanently associated with this group. Countless modern roses have the wonderful "damask" fragrance that originated in this class.

Just as gallicas were cherished by northern Europeans for their beauty and medicinal properties, damasks were similarly loved (and used) by the people

"English" roses display old rose–style blooms on repeat-blooming shrubs. 'Munstead Wood', shown here, is evocative of the original gallica roses.

of the ancient Middle East, as well as those in present-day Iran, Iraq, Turkey, and Pakistan.

Although the damasks are mostly once-bloomers like the gallicas, one variety, the appropriately named 'Autumn Damask', will flower twice yearly: first in late spring and again in late summer or early fall. No other Euro-Mediterranean roses have this ability, so the question of how 'Autumn Damask' acquired it mystified gardeners for centuries. (In the late twentieth century, the mystery was finally solved through genetic testing: the original damask rose is a cross between *R. gallica* and the repeat-blooming *Rosa moschata*, the musk rose from the western Himalayas. 'Autumn Damask' happened to express the normally recessive gene that allows for repeat-blooming. Of course, how a rose from the Himalayas made its way into ancient Syria is another mystery.)

Damasks usually form extremely thorny, sprawling shrubs. They are naturally heat tolerant thanks to their origins in the Middle East, and some can perform decently in South Florida if grafted properly (see chapter 2). Their once-blooming nature is their main liability.

ALBAS. No group of roses is more strongly associated with Medieval Europe than the albas. They are strongly tied to castle and monastery gardens; images of albas in such settings are found throughout artwork of the Middle Ages.

The first albas were wild crosses in northern Europe between damask roses and the native dog rose, *Rosa canina*, so-called because a tincture made from the roots would supposedly cure rabies from a dog bite. Alba roses have handsome gray-green foliage on large, upright to climbing shrubs but bloom only in shades of white or pale pink ("alba" is Latin for "white"). The flowers generally have a sensuous floral perfume.

R. canina is another once-blooming species, as are her alba rose descendants. Roses in this class are remarkably cold tolerant, thriving as far north

The sensuously perfumed, pure white flowers of 'Brian Michael' are reminiscent of the old alba roses but bloom all year long in South Florida.

as Scandinavia with no winter protection, but they fail in South Florida's tropical heat.

CENTIFOLIAS. Latin for "hundred-petaled," the centifolias are the roses immortalized by the Dutch and Flemish painters of the 1600s. Also called cabbage roses because of their immense, full flowers, the original centifolia rose (simply called 'Centifolia') was developed as a backcross between an alba and a damask by Dutch nurseryman John van Hogheland around 1591. Its double flowers were completely sterile, but a fertile, single-flowered mutation appeared in 1769 that allowed new centifolias to be bred.

Although they are once-bloomers like the albas, centifolias became adored for their powerfully sweet fragrances; they are still heavily used by the French perfume industry today for this reason. Colors include shades of white, pink, and purplish crimson. Because the flowers are so large, the canes tend to arch under their weight.

As with the albas, centifolias grow and flower poorly in South Florida.

MOSS ROSES. One interesting aspect of the centifolias was their tendency to produce mutations with a thick growth of soft, balsam-scented glands covering the unopened flower buds and stems. Sometimes entire canes could be covered with this adorable mossy growth, which was usually reddish to brownish and gave the whole plant a special tactile quality—you just want to rub it like bubble wrap!

The appropriately named moss roses were soon set apart from the centifolias. They were beloved by the Victorians in the late 1800s, with dozens of varieties created during that time, but the group itself wasn't used to develop any new classes.

Recently, however, Oregon breeder Paul Barden has ignited renewed interest in this group by developing a new line of "modern" moss roses that come in a wide color range; many have dependable rebloom on heat-tolerant plants. I myself have yet to trial these new moss roses in South Florida.

The East Asian Roses

Only two distinct classes of East Asian roses are present. In contrast to the Euro-Mediterranean roses, their flowers are smaller and less fragrant, but the shrubs are naturally adapted to tropical growing conditions.

CHINAS. According to the famous rosarian Graham Stuart Thomas, China roses are the foundation of all modern roses. *Rosa chinensis*, the spe-

"Sports" are spontaneous mutations that randomly occur on rosebushes. Here, dark pink 'Belinda's Dream' sports to the much paler 'Belinda's Blush'.

cies behind this class, possesses the most coveted of all rose traits: remontancy, the ability for a rosebush to bloom more than once annually. Gardeners worldwide owe a big debt of gratitude to the "Four Stud Chinas" that were brought to France in the early 1800s: 'Parson's Pink China', 'Slater's Crimson China', 'Hume's Blush Tea-Scented China', and 'Park's Yellow Tea-Scented China'. These four roses would become the fathers of every modern repeat-blooming rose in existence.

Compared to the Euro-Mediterranean roses, the flowers of China roses are smaller and less shapely, with loose, shaggy petals. Where they blow the European roses away, however, is in their remontancy. China roses will rebloom continuously throughout the year unless a freeze puts a stop to new vegetative

The bright chartreuse fronds of the giant king fern (*Angiopteris evecta*) contrast dramatically with the dark greens and reds of the famous China rose 'Louis-Philippe'.

growth—a far cry from the gallicas, damasks, albas, centifolias, and mosses, which all only bloom for about a month every year.

China roses' fragrances tend to be earthy and peppery rather than floral or tangy. Their shrubs are dense and rounded, with twiggy canes and slender leaflets. One unusual trait of the Chinas is their tendency to "suntan"—their petals actually darken as they age, unlike those of Euro-Mediterranean roses that tend to fade as they age.

As *R. chinensis* is native to the humid subtropics of Southeast Asia, the China roses are all perfectly suited to the similar climate of South Florida. Flowers come in shades of white, pink, and red, including true scarlet and ruby tones not found in the Euro-Mediterranean roses.

TEAS. Also originating in subtropical Asia are the tea roses. There are two legends behind the quirky name. The first claims it was because of the flowers' fragrance, comparable to a fresh cup of Chinese black tea (my nose agrees). The second says that the original specimens were sent to Europe in tea chests. Since there's no solid evidence proving one story over the other, pick whichever suits your fancy.

The teas originated as a cross between *R. chinensis* and *Rosa gigantea*, a huge climbing rose from the foothills of northeast India and Myanmar. This created a group of roses with shrubs larger, leafier, and more graceful than the Chinas—as well as more cold sensitive. Their correspondingly larger blooms would often nod or dangle because they were too heavy for their slender stalks. As with the Chinas, most tea roses bloom throughout the year unless halted by frost.

The *R. gigantea* genes added a few other changes: petal edges that curl back to create pointed tips (the prototype of our modern florists' roses) and a

'Duchesse de Brabant', an everblooming tea rose, teams up with 'Rockin'® Deep Purple' salvia to hide the entrance to a secret garden.

pale lemon color that led to a broader color range of pastel cream, beige, and warm seashell pink.

As Europeans developed tea roses in the early 1800s, gardeners saw the rise of a class notable for everblooming, pastel-colored flowers on elegant but cold-sensitive shrubs reserved strictly for greenhouses and, by proxy, the rich who could afford them. Thus, the tea roses were the horticultural Ferraris of their day, the province of the upper class.

Today, tea roses have lost their initial haughtiness but retained all their charm. These are veritable superstars in humid subtropical to fully tropical gardens; most are beautiful and extremely disease-resistant roses in South Florida.

East Meets West: The Reblooming Old Roses

The next four classes represent the first blending of rose genetics from the East (Chinas and teas) with those grown in Europe at the time (primarily gallicas, damasks, albas, and centifolias). All are reblooming to some degree.

PORTLANDS (DAMASK PERPETUALS). Portland roses originated in neither Oregon nor Maine; the group was named for their first envoy, 'Duchess of Portland', which was bred in Italy in the late 1700s. Originally thought to be a cross between 'Autumn Damask' and 'Slater's Crimson China', recent DNA analysis has shown that 'Duchess of Portland' is actually a cross between 'Autumn Damask' and *R. gallica*. Because 'Autumn Damask' features prominently in their breeding, the group is sometimes called "damask perpetuals."

Both in numbers and stature, the Portlands are a small group. Fewer than 50 varieties were created at their peak in the early 1800s, and all are low-growing shrubs seldom taller than 4', even in hot climates. They rebloom throughout the year, albeit somewhat erratically, in shades of pink, crimson, and magenta; their sweet fragrances tend to be strong and damasky. Portlands are also notable for having short flower stalks with foliage growing right up to the flower buds—what Graham Stuart Thomas affectionately called a "shoulder of leaves."

Portland roses perform acceptably well in South Florida, especially if grafted properly (see chapter 2) and sited to receive afternoon shade.

BOURBONS. Another class with a misleading name, Bourbon roses have nothing to do with the potent potable. They originated on the Isle of Bourbon (now called Réunion), a tropical island off the coast of Madagascar that was a popular rest stop for ships traveling between Europe and Asia in the 1800s.

In those days, agricultural fields on the island were hedged with roses, particularly 'Autumn Damask' and 'Parson's Pink China'. Around 1820, a local farmer stumbled across a new rose growing in his hedges that appeared to be a cross between the two. He showed it to a visiting French botanist, who collected seeds and cuttings of the plant and sent them to Paris. From there, the Bourbon class was born à la Française.

The Bourbon class is one of extremes. Shrubs may be very short (barely 3') or rampantly tall; rebloom can be nonexistent or nonstop; fragrances range

Compact, prolific, and fragrant, 'Souvenir de St. Anne's' makes a wonderful Bourbon rose for small gardens.

from mild to decadent. Colors include shades of white, pink, red, and magenta, as well as several striped combinations.

Despite their tropical origins, Bourbons are very hit or miss in South Florida. Some varieties ('Maggie', 'Souvenir de St. Anne's') are phenomenal, heavy-blooming, disease-resistant roses here while others are the exact opposite. Be leery of any Bourbon roses not specifically mentioned as performing well in South Florida.

NOISETTES. The Noisette class is one that we Americans can truly call our own. In 1802, John Champneys, a rice farmer in Charleston, South Carolina, crossed 'Parson's Pink China' with *R. moschata*, the aforementioned musk rose. The result was a compact, repeat-flowering climber with huge clusters of small, spicily fragrant flowers. Charleston gardeners quickly fell in love with 'Champneys' Pink Cluster', including Champneys' neighbor, Philippe Noisette.

Philippe raised a seedling of 'Champneys' Pink Cluster' even lovelier than the original and sent cuttings of this new rose to his brother, Louis Noisette, in France. Louis then proudly introduced 'Blush Noisette' around Paris to much applause. Thus, the Noisette class began with dual "flagships" in both the United States and France.

American Noisettes tended to follow the 'Champneys' Pink Cluster' model: short, bushy climbers with small flowers in massive clusters, primarily in shades of white, pink, and red. The French, however, began crossing Noisettes with newly imported tea roses. This created a tea-Noisette subclass with larger flowers in smaller clusters and a wider color range that included pastel tints of buff and salmon from the teas. The tea-Noisettes were also substantially larger plants, forming heavy climbers often 20' or more in spread.

Noisettes (most notably the tea-Noisettes) are cold-tender, heat-tolerant roses that do very well overall in South Florida. Most of them (again, notably the tea-Noisettes) are also powerfully fragrant, with aromas ranging from the peppery scents of the Chinas to the more floral scents of Euro-Mediterranean roses. Like the Portlands, many Noisettes prefer morning sun and afternoon shade.

HYBRID PERPETUALS. Hybrid perpetuals were the last class of old roses created before their famous descendants, the hybrid teas, crept onto the scene. They were superstars in their heyday, which began around 1840 and lasted until 1900; over 4,000 cultivars were created during that time.

Many roses, like the Noisette 'Haywood Hall', are pollinator magnets, perfect to include in to-day's bee-friendly landscaping.

As tea roses became a status symbol of wealthy Europeans—only the wealthy could afford the greenhouses necessary to keep them alive through the winter—a market emerged for "middle class" roses that were reliably cold hardy outdoors *sans* greenhouse. The hybrid perpetuals filled that market. The first half of their name was accurate: their ancestry was more "hybrid" than any other group back then. If you took a blender, threw in genetic material from virtually every other rose class (particularly the gallicas, damasks, and Bourbons), and then hit "purée," the result would be a hybrid perpetual.

"Perpetual," unfortunately, was much *less* accurate. As a group, hybrid perpetuals were not consistent rebloomers, and many varieties had no rebloom at all. Additionally, the shrubs themselves were actually unattractive, with chunky, sparsely foliaged canes forming stiff, clumsy plants—quite the opposite of the graceful, leafy teas.

To compensate for these shortcomings, breeders of hybrid perpetuals focused on creating varieties with larger, more individually spectacular flowers. This led to the world's first rose competition, held in London in July 1858, where both amateur and professional gardeners showed off big, beautiful, bountiful blooms against each other.

Hybrid perpetuals are still grown today, though their current popularity is but a shadow of their former glory. As with the Bourbons, some varieties—'Marchesa Boccella', for example—perform wonderfully here while others struggle.

ROSE CLASSES—MODERN ROSES

HYBRID TEAS. When French breeder Jean-Baptiste Guillot debuted a pink rose called 'La France' in 1867, it didn't create a massive wave in the gardening world. But she was an interesting new rose nonetheless, with physical traits exactly halfway between her tea and hybrid perpetual parents. She was more cold hardy than a tea rose and more everblooming than a hybrid perpetual—and these selling points would later become the tagline of a colossal new dynasty.

Though the hybrid teas were technically established with 'La France' in 1867, the class didn't take off in either numbers or popularity until 1900. That was when Joseph Pernet-Ducher debuted 'Soleil D'or', a cross between 'Antoine Ducher', a magenta hybrid perpetual, and 'Persian Yellow', a double form of the wild Austrian briar rose (*Rosa foetida*). The resultant seedling, 'Soleil D'or', produced large antique-style blooms of deep bronzy yellow.

Although not a hybrid tea itself, 'Soleil D'or' hybridized readily with them—and introduced new color genes into their lineage. Suddenly, the hybrid tea class had one unbeatable ace up their sleeve: exotic new colors that no other class had.

Prior to 'Soleil D'or', roses primarily bloomed in shades of white, pink, and red—lovely, but rather tired and passé. Now, the hybrid tea class had every conceivable shade of yellow, gold, orange, bronze, apricot, and copper in

The fragrant and prolific hybrid tea 'Flo Nelson' pumps out soft orange blooms that harmonize perfectly with tropical crotons and bromeliads.

their palette—and eventually, even lavender, gray, and brown. And as if those new hues weren't enough, the 'Soleil D'or' genes also allowed for multicolored blends of every new color *and* every old color. Want a lavender rose edged in red? A pink and yellow bicolor? Orange with brown shading? The possibilities were infinite.

It's easy to imagine the mad rush that followed: suddenly, every rose breeder wanted in on the hybrid tea game, and the group exploded in numbers exponentially. The earlier rose classes were almost forgotten entirely. Soon, even the original tea/hybrid perpetual crossing protocol became obsolete: hybrid teas were simply inbred with each other over and over as breeders raced to outdo one another in the frenzied pursuit of the Best Rose Ever.

Today, hybrid teas are the dominant class when you step into a nursery, visit a florist, or browse an online retailer. Of the 25,000-odd rose varieties currently in existence, over 10,000 are hybrid teas. Their appeal largely rests with their iconic silhouette: a single, large, high-centered flower held aloft on a long, stiff stem, which fits the most common concept of what a "rose" should look like.

As with their hybrid perpetual ancestors, the shrubs themselves tend to be stiff and ungainly. Every color of the rainbow except for true blue is now found in their ranks. Their suitability for South Florida is as varied as their numbers: some bloom heavily here while others never flower.

POLYANTHAS. A separate project Guillot developed around the time of 'La France' was the polyanthas. Their first representative, 'Paquerette', was a cross between dwarf forms of *R. chinensis* and *Rosa multiflora*, the Japanese wild rose now infamous throughout the temperate United States as a highly invasive weed. (The great American nurseryman Michael Dirr once wrote that if you intentionally plant *R. multiflora*, do so with the knowledge that none of your neighbors will ever speak to you again.)

The resulting crosses became known as the polyanthas. Greek for "many-flowered," they exhibited the best traits of both parents: remontancy from *R. chinensis*; extreme hardiness and large flower clusters from *R. multiflora*. Although individual polyantha flowers are small (typically just 1" in diameter), the shrubs bloom so heavily that a single plant at the height of a flower flush can be a drench of pure color in the landscape—a step up from the average rosebush featuring spots of color on a mostly green plant.

Polyanthas are still widely grown today; they generally form low-growing, sprawling shrubs and bloom in a wide color range like the hybrid teas. Most perform well in South Florida. They are especially loved by professional landscapers for their everblooming, low-maintenance nature.

FLORIBUNDAS. As the polyanthas grew in number, breeders noted that their only real drawback was the small size of the individual blossoms. Naturally, the obvious solution was to cross them with something that was larger

Drifts of the everblooming polyantha 'La Marne' and golden yellow thryallis dress up this rock garden in Miami.

flowered, came in a range of colors, and had remontancy genes already in place. And for those traits, the obvious group to turn to was the hybrid teas.

The first such cross was 'Gruss an Aachen', produced by German breeder Wilhelm Hinner in 1909. In nearby Denmark, the prestigious Poulsen family of rose growers took Hinner's prototype further, creating a whole line of "hybrid polyanthas" that had larger, hybrid tea-shaped flowers but produced with a polyantha's abundance.

The Poulsens' creations in the early 1920s—'Else Poulsen', 'Rödhätte' ('Red Riding Hood'), and 'Kirsten Poulsen'—were all commercially successful. Across the Atlantic, the expanding American company of Jackson & Perkins seized the polyantha/hybrid tea model and made their own line of releases. Realizing that this new group needed their own name—the larger flowers and more upright shrubs were too divergent from "regular" polyanthas—Jackson & Perkins coined the term "floribunda" (the Latin translation of "polyantha") in the 1930s.

With its sweet licorice fragrance, floribunda 'Julia Child' flowers prolifically all year round in South Florida, perfect for dressing up a front walkway.

Floribundas are still as popular today as when they first began 100 years ago. Aside from the fact that they are generally shorter plants with clustered flowers, they are otherwise similar to hybrid teas in terms of color range, flower shape, and varied suitability for South Florida.

GRANDIFLORAS. In 1954, American horticulturist Dr. Walter E. Lammerts successfully crossed a hybrid tea with a floribunda. The result was 'Queen Elizabeth', a lovely pink rose that flowered with a floribunda's profusion but formed a very tall shrub more vigorous than either parent. Predictably, other breeders caught on and began making their own hybrid tea/floribunda crosses.

The resulting class, the grandifloras, can basically be thought of as floribundas on steroids. They produce branched clusters of flowers like the floribundas but with long flower stems like the hybrid teas; the plants themselves are larger and bulkier than either floribunda or hybrid tea shrubs.

Spurred on by the popularity of 'Queen Elizabeth', the grandifloras enjoyed a heyday from the 1950s through the 1980s, with hundreds of cultivars released during that time. The group's popularity has faded in recent decades, however—consumers nowadays seem to prefer roses that are clearly either floribundas or hybrid teas, rather than a little of each. And as with the two parent classes, grandifloras' performance in South Florida varies per individual.

The huge, shapely flowers of 'Mother of Pearl', one of the best grandifloras for South Florida, look smashing with other warm colors, like these 'Mission Giant Yellow' marigolds.

MINIATURES AND MINIFLORAS. The miniature roses of today's grocery store florists, usually wrapped in some sort of garish colored foil, got their start in Switzerland around 1917. As the story goes, Swiss botanist Henry Correvon was informed by his army friend, Colonel Roulet, of a tiny, everblooming rose growing in various window boxes in the Swiss village of Mauborjet.

The rose, named 'Rouletti' in honor of her discoverer, was a true miniature form of *R. chinensis* that stayed under 2' tall without trimming with correspondingly tiny leaves and flowers. Correvon sent plants of 'Rouletti' on to various hybridizers, who crossed them with the newly emergent hybrid teas and floribundas, and a race of miniature roses was born.

Fast-forward to 1970s Maryland. Another military man—this time, former U.S. soldier J. Benjamin Williams—began dabbling in rose breeding after retiring from service in World War II. By 1973, Williams had developed several beautiful floribunda/miniature crosses. Unfortunately, his new creations had a problem: per the American Rose Society's (ARS) guidelines, they were too small to be considered floribundas, but too large to be miniatures. Williams pestered the ARS over and over for a new designation for his collection of semidwarfs, which he called "minifloras." The ARS finally relented in 1999, and miniflora became the latest new rose classification.

Today, miniatures and minifloras are essentially just pint-sized versions of hybrid teas and floribundas, found in all colors and color combinations, and with similarly varying degrees of performance in South Florida.

SHRUB ROSES. Ever since roses first came into cultivation, countless varieties have not fit neatly into any of the aforementioned classes. As humans cannot help but categorize, we gave these lovable misfits their own moniker. "Shrub roses" is a nebulous term designed to encompass any rose that can't be pigeonholed into any other class.

Over time, notable distinctions have separated out various subclasses of shrub roses. The two most relevant to South Florida gardens are the hybrid musks and the English roses.

Hybrid musks began as the retirement project of British reverend Joseph Hardwick Pemberton, whose family had grown roses commercially since the late 1800s. In the early 1900s, Pemberton crossed *R. moschata* with a reblooming form of *R. multiflora*. After adding teas and hybrid teas into the mix, he developed a new group of roses unified by a graceful semiclimbing

The misfit "shrub roses" often resemble roses from other classes. Here, 'Helga's Quest' shows off hybrid tea-esque flowers at Florida Southern College in Lakeland.

habit; handsome, disease-resistant foliage; and everblooming, musk-scented flowers in a range of soft pastels.

English roses, as their name implies, were also started in Great Britain. Beginning in the late 1960s, Shropshire nurseryman David Austin had a dream of reigniting interest in the romantic, once-blooming Euro-Mediterranean roses (primarily gallicas, albas, and centifolias) by crossing them with hybrid teas and floribundas to make them remontant. His line of English roses (sometimes called "David Austin roses"), which now number in the hundreds, have exquisitely perfumed, antique-shaped flowers that rebloom throughout the year in a broad color palette.

Hybrid musks and English roses are among the best shrub roses for South

Florida; most grow vigorously and flower heavily here. A handful from each group need winter chill to flower well; those varieties are naturally excluded from this book.

CLIMBERS. All roses are considered shrubs, but many grow as scandent, or "climbing," shrubs: they have long, flexible stems that climb up and over nearby objects using their thorns as hooks. (Scandent shrubs differ from

Garden arches and climbing roses are a match made in heaven; here, 'Prosperity's white blooms combine with purple datura, red coleus, and cardboard palm (*Zamia furfuracea*).

true vines like wisteria or mandevilla, whose stems actually twine around objects.)

Climbing roses are found in many of the old roses, especially albas, teas, Bourbons, and Noisettes. In most cases this is because one of the founding species of the class was naturally scandent in nature, like *R. moschata* or *R. gigantea*. Spontaneous mutations (sports) are another source of climbing roses, especially in modern roses. Simply put, a regular "bush" version of a rose—for example, the hybrid tea 'Peace'—will suddenly form long, snaking canes unlike any that the plant normally produces. Thus, the "bush" version of 'Peace' has sported into a climbing mutation of itself ('Climbing Peace', usually abbreviated as 'Cl. Peace').

Climbing roses' suitability for South Florida vacillates more than any other class, particularly where sports are concerned. For example, the "bush" version of the polyantha 'Cécile Brunner' blooms wonderfully in South Florida, but the climbing sport rarely flowers here and should therefore be avoided. Meanwhile, 'Peace' displays the exact opposite problem for us: the "bush" version blooms poorly while the climbing sport blooms well here.

EARTH-KIND®. Although technically not a separate class, Earth-Kind® roses are increasingly viewed as one by both growers and consumers alike.

Beginning in the late 1980s, Dr. Steve George of Texas A&M University spearheaded an ambitious project: to designate a group of roses that could thrive as healthy, beautiful landscape plants without excess water, fertilizers, or chemicals. George's team accomplished this by trialing different varieties, each over an eight-year period, in diverse locations throughout Texas to ensure a broad range of soil, water, and microclimate conditions.

Dr. George's Earth-Kind® roses now include about 30 varieties so hardy and easy to grow that they are suitable for even the most novice gardener. Representatives from several classes, both old and modern, are present. New varieties are added regularly as the project continues their trials.

Many Earth-Kind® roses bloom well in South Florida, and several are included in this compendium (see chapter 4).

2

The South Florida Rose

In May 2007 I relocated from Maryland to South Florida to work as a designer with a prestigious Miami-based landscape company. And as soon as I became a new transplant here, I was dumbstruck by the reluctance of South Floridians to even *think* about growing roses.

After talking with countless people in South Florida over the years, there seem to be three big misconceptions contributing to this hesitation:

1. Roses are so strongly associated with cold-climate gardens that they can't possibly adapt to more tropical growing conditions.
2. In northern gardens, roses usually suffer from various pests and diseases that are kept in check with an annual winter dormancy. Since South Florida has no such winter dormancy, pests and diseases must be rampant here.
3. Root-knot nematodes—tiny wormlike creatures that kill rosebushes by slowly strangling their roots—are so prevalent in South Florida's sandy soils that this problem alone prohibits growing roses.

Fortunately, I can debunk all three myths right now.

First: While many roses do need some winter chill to flower well, just as many varieties actually flower *better* in South Florida's warm climate—all year long in most cases. These include dozens of old roses and just as many modern roses. Almost no other part of the continental United States can boast the ability to enjoy these wonderful flowers 12 months a year as we here can.

Next: While South Florida roses do have some pests, many of the worst offenders are entirely nonexistent here. Japanese beetles, which decimate roses

One of the healthiest hybrid teas for South Florida, 'St. Patrick's yellow flowers hover above a mass of scarlet pentas.

in northern parts of the country, can't survive in South Florida. The same goes for powdery mildew, a major fungal disease in the dry western states: in over 15 years, I've never observed a case of powdery mildew on roses here, as our humidity discourages this disease. Gophers and deer—serious rose predators in colder zones—are also a non-issue for us.

Finally, to tackle the root-knot nematodes, I proudly present our silver bullet: 'Fortuniana' rootstock.

'FORTUNIANA' ROOTSTOCK

Many roses, especially modern hybrids, grow best when grafted onto a strong root system, or "rootstock." Over time, two rootstocks in particular have become popular with rose growers because of their vigor: 'Dr. Huey' and 'Multiflora'. Unfortunately, both grow poorly in tropical climates, and both are susceptible to root-knot nematodes.

But a third rootstock—that of *Rosa* × 'Fortuniana', a once-blooming white rose discovered in subtropical China in the 1840s—is fully resistant to root-knot nematodes. The little beasts simply find the roots of 'Fortuniana' unpalatable. Additionally, 'Fortuniana' is naturally tolerant of seasonal drought, humid heat, and sandy soils—in other words, the overall growing conditions of South Florida!

A good handful of old roses (mostly Chinas, teas, and Noisettes, as well as a few Portlands and Bourbons) are naturally nematode-resistant. If planted and tended well, they can usually survive as own-root shrubs in South Florida. For modern roses, however—the hybrid teas, floribundas, English roses, and so forth—planting only 'Fortuniana'-grafted plants is necessary to ensure that they are safeguarded against nematode attacks.

Rosa × 'Fortuniana'

It's un-"Fortun-"-nate that 'Fortuniana' was given such an awkward name. Sadder still is this rose's seldom being thought of except as a root system for other roses. But 'Fortuniana' actually makes a wonderful South Florida garden plant!

Although there's but one annual bloom period, 'Fortuniana's floral displays can last for up to three months, typically from January through March. The pure white, double, pompon-shaped flowers have a tight button eye and emit a delicious violet-like perfume; the shrub itself forms a handsome mass of arching canes, splendid as either a freestanding shrub or a climber. 'Fortuniana's unique foliage—trifoliate, diamond-shaped leaflets of an especially bright glossy green—is also completely disease-free in our climate.

For gardeners open-minded enough to consider a once-blooming shrub in their yard, 'Fortuniana' will prove to be dependable, low-maintenance, eco-friendly, and simply beautiful.

The arching, informal growth of 'Fortuniana' makes a wonderful climbing rose or sprawling shrub; the specimen here was used to hide an unsightly shed.

SOUTH FLORIDA'S CLIMATE: SUBTROPICAL
OR FULLY TROPICAL?

Is South Florida's climate subtropical or fully tropical? The answer is somewhere in the middle—what I term a "quasi-tropical" climate.

Strictly speaking, all of Florida is subtropical because it lies outside the two boundaries of the tropics (the Tropic of Cancer and the Tropic of Capricorn). However, a climate map of North America shows that the subtropical zone includes everything from southern Virginia through Florida and westward into Texas. Although technically true, this gross oversimplification would make it seem like gardening in Naples is the same as gardening in Nashville—obviously, this isn't the case.

Furthermore, Florida's year-round climate gets noticeably more tropical

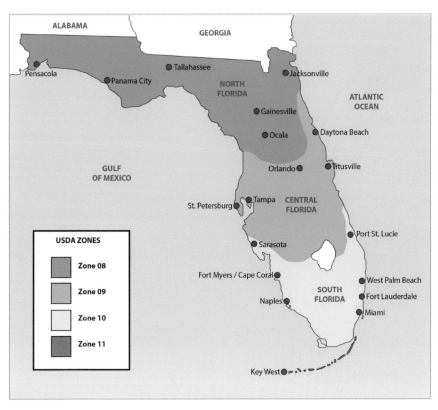

Distinctions among the growing zones of Florida indicated by color: dark green for North Florida, light green for Central Florida, and yellow and orange for South Florida.

immediately south of Lake Okeechobee. This is because South Florida is surrounded by warm marine water on three sides (the Atlantic Ocean to the east and south, the Gulf of Mexico to the west). The constant barrage of warm, moist air elevates South Florida from a subtropical climate into a more fully tropical one. Proof of this lies in our plant species: coconut palms and other fully tropical plants, which can't survive the winter in a subtropical zone, flourish here.

However—and here's where things get muddled—because even southern-most Florida is still north of the Tropic of Cancer, we aren't as 100 percent tropical as, say, the Amazon Rainforest. Freezes, and even snowfall, can (and do) occur here. Thus, we're quasi-tropical: more tropical than North or Central Florida, but still not quite "truly" tropical.

Confused? Worry not! Regardless of our neither-here-nor-there climate, growing roses in South Florida is surprisingly straightforward.

GROWING ROSES IN SOUTH FLORIDA

Step 1: Site Selection

Before you pick up a shovel, the first step is to analyze your yard and ensure that your existing conditions can accommodate roses.

Roses are sun lovers by nature, and they need a minimum of six hours of direct sun each day. A few varieties tolerate (or even enjoy) light or partial shade, but none will succeed in full, dark shade. Select a location in full sun, at least 6–8' away from any small trees and 15' or more from large trees. This will ensure your roses aren't shaded by overhead canopies and that their water and nutrients aren't siphoned off by aggressive tree roots.

The best soil for roses is good garden loam: rich in organic matter and evenly moist but well drained. Avoid permanently wet, marshy soils as well as bone-dry locations beyond the reach of irrigation.

Step 2: Choosing Roses

Once a suitable area is picked, it's time to choose the roses you want to grow. (See chapter 4 for a list of 100 good varieties and chapter 5 for a list of retailers.)

This is sometimes the hardest part of the process because roses generally grow bigger here than in colder climates—and unless you have acres of land (regretfully, I do not), sooner or later you'll run out of space.

Also called 'Josephine Land', 'Heritage' has sweetly fragrant, camellia-shaped blooms on a shrub tolerant of partial shade.

Be realistic with how many plants your space can fit. Roses need good air circulation among individual plants and should never be crowded; a good rule of thumb is to plant most varieties 4' on center (each plant's center 4' away from the next). The idea of having 20 different varieties in one bed may sound lovely, but if your space can only fit half that many, edit the list down to your top choices.

Step 3: Planting

What time of year is best for planting roses in South Florida? Different growers have different opinions on this, but I advocate planting (or transplanting) roses only between November and March. The cooler, milder temperatures will ensure that minimal stress is placed on the plant's root system as it establishes itself. Roses planted in the heat of midsummer run the risk of succumbing to potentially fatal transplant shock.

For planting new rosebushes, excavate holes; backfill with good-quality compost mix; then position plants in their final locations to get beautiful results like the 'Granada' shown here.

For each plant, dig a hole about 20" across and 16" deep. Discard three-quarters of the excavated soil, and mix the remaining with a blend of equal parts topsoil, composted manure, and peat moss. Begin backfilling the hole, firming down the soil as you go.

Remove the rose from its pot. Place it in the partially filled hole such that the rose's soil line will be level with the finished soil level of the bed. Never bury a rosebush deeper than its current container level nor leave it exposed high above the bed's finished grade.

Next, finish filling the hole with your soil blend, making sure to pack it down firmly to eliminate air pockets. Water each plant gently with a hose for a good 60 seconds. If you notice substantial runoff, mound up a small ring of soil around the outer perimeter of the plant to keep water near its root zone.

Step 4: Watering

Newly planted roses should be watered daily, especially during hot or dry weather, for the first four weeks. Afterwards, as the plant becomes established, watering can be tapered down.

For watering your roses, you can either hand water with a hose or use an irrigation system. Hand watering is, of course, the simplest option—a good garden hose can be bought for $50 or less—but also the most time consuming, as each rosebush needs about 60 seconds of irrigation. For small gardens this works fine, but for larger landscapes, an irrigation system is more practical.

Although sprinkler-type irrigation systems are the most common in South Florida, drip irrigation is infinitely better for roses. As the name implies, a drip system uses a network of small, flexible pipes along the soil surface to drip water directly into a plant's root zone.

Drip systems are typically more expensive to install than conventional sprinklers, but their benefits far outweigh the price tag. Water is delivered directly onto a rose's roots, which eliminates runoff and will lower your water bill over time. The reduced runoff also ensures that soil nutrients don't leach out of the ground rapidly. And because drip irrigation doesn't wet a rose's foliage, fungal diseases like blackspot are greatly controlled.

For both sprinkler systems and drip systems, roses do best with about 30 minutes of irrigation twice weekly during our cool season (December through April) and three times a week during the hot season (heavy rains notwithstanding).

Step 5: Fertilizing

Roses are heavy feeders, and South Florida's sandy soils are generally poor and devoid of nutrients. A fertilizing program is therefore necessary here.

The three essential nutrients roses need to survive are nitrogen (N), phosphorus (P), and potassium (K). Prepackaged fertilizers usually have this "N-P-K" ratio indicated on their packaging. Roses in South Florida tend to do

Roses and bananas are excellent garden playmates: both enjoy lots of sun, rich soil, and consistent irrigation. Here, 'Lyda Rose' weaves her airy blossoms into a backyard banana grove.

best with nitrogen slightly higher than phosphorus or potassium because our heavy rains cause nitrogen to leach out of the ground faster than the other two elements.

Most garden centers stock slow-release synthetic fertilizers that can be applied every few months in South Florida per the manufacturer's instructions. For a more sustainable approach, many organic options are available. These include composted manure (nitrogen, some phosphorus, and potassium); alfalfa pellets (nitrogen and some potassium); blood meal (nitrogen and potassium); fish emulsion (nitrogen); bone meal (phosphorus); and greensand (potassium).

Additionally, two other organic nutrients good to have are Epsom salts and chelated iron. Because South Florida's soils are generally both alkaline and nutrient poor, roses frequently develop a nutrient deficiency called chlorosis; the telltale sign is sickly, yellowish-white leaves with green veins. Epsom salts and chelated iron both help to correct this problem. Powdered sulfur can also be used to directly acidify your soil. For all of these nutrients, consult the manufacturer's instructions for how to apply them.

For gardeners interested in adopting a completely organic feeding protocol, the best program I could recommend was created by longtime South Florida rose lover Connie Vierbicky, whose Sarasota garden has the most magnificent roses I've ever seen.

Step 6: Pruning

Pruning seems to be the single most confusing aspect of rose maintenance, simply based on how often I get questions about it. Let's simplify things!

In South Florida, pruning is done for four reasons: to remove dead or diseased growth; to shorten an overgrown plant; to rejuvenate old plants; or to encourage larger flowers during the cool season. In all cases, use a pair of sharp secateurs (pruning shears with curved blades) for cutting canes ½" or less in diameter. For thicker canes, use bypass loppers or a pruning saw.

Removing dead or diseased canes can be done any time of year in South Florida. Simply cut out the damaged growth back to where it meets a thick, healthy cane. If the whole cane is sickly, remove it completely.

Shortening an overgrown rosebush can also be done year round. Starting at the plant's extremities, remove any skinny, twiggy growth. Gradually work your way inward until no more than a third of the plant has been trimmed. Remove any branches that cross or rub against each other as you go.

Table 1. Connie Vierbicky's Organic Rose Feeding Schedule

Time of Year	Product	Amount	Notes
January/March/May/July/September/November	Epsom salt	½ cup	Spread around each plant; water well. Use 50% less for smaller plants.
	Milorganite	2 cups	
	Gypsum	1 cup	
February/May/November	Dehydrated fat-free milk	4 cups	Mix MaxiCrop powder in bucket of hot water. Add remaining products and mix well; pour into 30+ gallon garbage can; fill can with water. Use 1 gallon per plant. Rinse foliage thoroughly after applying, and water each plant additionally to ensure solution soaks through completely.
	Fish emulsion	2 cups	
	MaxiCrop 1–0–4 (dehydrated seaweed)	½ cup	
	Epsom salts		
February/August	Jim Young's Purely Organic fertilizer mix (available at www.PurelyOrganicFertilizer.com)	3 cups	Spread around each plant; water well.
April/October	Organic alfalfa pellets	2 cups	Spread around plant; mix gently into soil; water well.
Once per month	Langbeinite (Sul-Po-Mag)	¼ cup to ½ cup	Spread around plant; use less for smaller plants, more for larger plants; water well.

Rejuvenation pruning is best performed from November through March, so that new growth can luxuriate in our mild cool season. Follow the same instructions as for shortening an overgrown rosebush, but also remove any canes thinner than a pencil. Once all twiggy growth is gone, the plant should have only its largest, thickest canes remaining. Next, evenly remove about half of these canes, so that the plant is opened up. Finally, shorten these remaining canes by two-thirds. This process will encourage the plant to begin producing vigorous new shoots from its base.

Last, many modern roses (particularly hybrid teas, floribundas, grandifloras, and English roses) will produce their biggest and most shapely flowers on new growth produced during our cool season. For these varieties, give them a rejuvenation-style pruning (see above) in November or December, but shorten existing growth only by half instead of two-thirds.

The mother of 'Archduke Charles', 'Old Blush' produces heavy sprays of lilac-pink flowers off and on throughout the year.

'Peggy Martin', an easy and heat-tolerant climber from New Orleans, ornaments a dramatic "moon gate" arbor in Fort Myers.

Climbing roses generally dislike periodic shortening of their growth for height reduction. Only select climbers whose mature size you can accommodate in your garden; beyond that, follow the same pruning guidelines as for "bush" roses with regard to removing dead or diseased growth.

PEST CONTROL

The idea that roses are fussy plants destined for failure because of countless pest problems is antiquated and untrue. In reality, most roses don't demand any more maintenance than any other garden flower.

As the saying goes, a dash of prevention is worth a pound of cure. With roses, pest prevention starts with common sense: select appropriate varieties (grafted on 'Fortuniana' if necessary); site and plant them well; and water and fertilize them, as you would any other landscape plant. Having a healthy, well-placed, well-grown rose will circumvent a lot of pest problems from the start.

But inevitably, there are a few nuisances that can attack even well-tended roses. I'll cover the most prevalent ones in South Florida and how best to handle them.

Balling

"Balling" occurs when excess rain or humidity cause rose blooms to turn brown and moldy as they're opening; occasionally, the condition is also triggered by *Botrytis* fungus. Balling is primarily a problem only with extremely double-flowered roses and, even then, only during our summer monsoons; it is virtually nonexistent during the cool season. Clip off "balled" flowers as they occur; to avoid the problem entirely, select single or semidouble cultivars. Cease® fungicide is a good organic treatment.

Blackspot

Irregular dark spots on foliage are the telltale signs of this common fungal disease; as it progresses, spots grow larger and leaves turn yellow and fall off. Although usually not fatal, blackspot results in weak, stunted plants that flower poorly as the plant devotes energy toward replacing dead leaves.

Blackspot spores are spread by splashing water during warm, humid weather. The disease is best managed by selecting resistant varieties and watering roses early in the morning so that the foliage dries quickly (a drip irrigation system is even better). For serious infections, use an organic spray like Cease® or a copper or sulfur fungicide.

Aphids

Aphids are small, bright green insects that cluster around flower buds and other tender new growth, distorting foliage and flowers as they feed; they also secrete a substance called "honeydew" that can cause sooty mold infections. Fortunately, aphids are generally easy to deal with: gently rub them off and smash them with your fingers, or (for the squeamish) knock them off with a sharp blast of water. For heavy infestations, natural predators such as ladybugs are effective, or try an organic insecticide such as Safer® insecticidal soap.

Spider Mites

More serious than aphids are spider mites, tiny arachnids that suck chlorophyll out of rose leaves; heavy infestations can weaken or kill plants. Drought-stressed bushes are most vulnerable, so keeping roses properly irrigated usu-

Clockwise from top left: Blackspot, a common fungal disease, appears as sooty splotches on leaves; chili thrips cause scorched-looking tip growth; chlorosis indicates nutrient deficiencies; "balling" is most often caused by hot, rainy weather.

ally avoids major attacks. Take action at the first sign of spider mite damage (leaves with brown or beige stippling and/or minute webbing). Organic treatments include insecticidal soaps like Safer®, horticultural oil, and releasing predatory mites that prey on spider mites. A sharp blast from the hose can also dislodge their nasty little colonies.

Chili Thrips

First seen in South Florida in 2005, these microscopic insects can kill entire rosebushes if left unchecked. Their calling card is shriveled flower buds and tip growth that looks as if scorched by fire. Chili thrips are extremely hard to control once they get established because they are too small for most insecticidal sprays to get at them. Two organic treatments that have shown promise, however, include Conserve® spray and the predatory mite species *Amblyseius swirskii*.

Rose Rosette Disease

Rose rosette disease (RRD) is a viral disease that first originated in western North America in the 1940s; its telltale sign is bizarre, mutated growth that is bright red and extremely thorny. The virus is spread by a tiny windborne mite; there is currently no cure, and infected plants always die within two years.

At the first sign of RRD, *immediately* dig up and double-bag the infected rosebush, roots and all. Dispose of it as far away from your garden as possible; do not compost it. Removing as many of the mites as possible is imperative to keep the virus from spreading.

While RRD is frightening, the good news is that currently it's extremely rare in South Florida.

Iguanas

Originally imported as pets, these voracious lizards are now a widespread invasive species throughout all of South Florida. They are exclusively herbivorous and consume the flowers, fruits, and tender vegetative growth of many different plants.

Because iguanas can both climb and swim, they are difficult to control via barriers. Their excrement is also laden with dangerous bacteria—so, while some view iguanas as cute little dinosaurs, they are not creatures you really want hanging around your yard.

Iguanas occasionally feed on roses but generally prefer other flowering plants, particularly hibiscus. The best means of protecting roses from iguanas starts by planting them far away from hibiscus—or better yet, not including hibiscus in your landscaping. Since iguanas are only active during the day, they can also be scared away—either by people or the family dog—but this requires regular action to be effective. For serious infestations, consider using specialized traps.

3

Landscaping with Roses

ARTISTRY

I always knew I wanted to be a garden designer someday. Ever since childhood, I've found it endlessly satisfying to arrange plants outdoors in the same manner that interior designers arrange furniture in a room—in both cases, giving someone's personal space a sense of function, pleasure, and above all, artistry.

It's in this latter capacity that roses truly excel: no other flower is more enjoyable to use for ornamenting an outdoor space. Moreover, that sense of enjoyment is mostly because the rose is a uniquely versatile garden plant,

'Vincent Godsiff', one of the "Bermuda mystery" roses, makes a beautiful privacy hedge for this front yard garden.

with almost endless variation in not just floral beauty but greenery as well. Roses range from petite miniatures to massive climbers; their shrubs can be stiff and formal or blousy and cascading; foliage textures range from dense to airy, and every conceivable shade of green is found in their leaves. Truly, roses have countless means of being designed into a landscape.

ROSE GARDEN VS. MIXED GARDEN

I am not a fan of rose gardens. Yes, you read that right.

That may sound like a bizarre thing for the author of a rose book to say. But before any confusion sets in, let me clarify: a rose garden in the "classic" sense is one where the only plants grown are roses, with little else in terms of plant diversity except for the turf pathways in between rose beds.

Rose gardens in that sense are increasingly becoming a relic of the past; even large public rose gardens are diversifying their roses with other plant species. As a professional garden designer, I especially support this new modality for residential landscapes.

A garden composed only of roses has two notable drawbacks: a lack of color when the roses are out of bloom and the monotony inherent even when the roses *are* in bloom. (This latter problem would be true of any single-species garden design—for example, imagine a residential garden composed only of hibiscus.)

Various roses and tropical flowers create a lovely cottage garden scene in Fort Lauderdale; included here are 'Duchesse de Brabant', 'Munstead Wood', and 'Poseidon'.

In a mixed garden, conversely, roses are merely one element in a wider range of species that includes annual and perennial flowers, shrubs, and even unconventional elements like ornamental grasses, vines, small trees or palms—even herbs and vegetables, if you refrain from using chemicals.

Although a mixed garden requires more thoughtful planning, and roses will be fewer since they must share space with other garden plants, there are several benefits to adopting this kind of design approach:

1. If the roses are ever out of bloom, color and texture are furnished by other garden plants.
2. The variety inherent in such a design generates a more exciting, dynamic, and multisensory garden experience to enjoy.
3. Including other plant species attractive to wildlife creates a more sustainable, eco-friendly design. Attracting beneficial insects can also help control some of the harmful ones.
4. Some plants actually mitigate rose pests all by themselves. Garlic chives (*Allium tuberosum*) inhibits blackspot spores; marigolds (*Tagetes spp.*) can repel nematodes; and Cuban oregano (*Plectranthus amboinicus*) can deter iguanas.

Roses for Special Situations: Pollinators

Today more than ever, bee-friendly garden choices are vital to the survival of these important insects. Roses are not often thought of as "pollinator" plants, but many are, in fact, highly attractive to bees. The following would all be splendid additions to a pollinator garden:

'Agrippina'	'Lyda Rose'
'Bermuda's Kathleen'	'Martha's Vineyard'
'Duchesse de Brabant'	'Nachitoches Noisette'
'Emmie Gray'	'Nur Mahal'
'Haywood Hall'	'Penelope'
'Iceberg'	'Vanity'
'Julia Child'	'Xander'
'La Marne'	'Yuki's Dream'

The wild rose–style blooms of 'Bermuda's Kathleen' look right at home in a planting of South Florida natives like slash pine and muhly grass.

A pastel garden scene is created with 'Vanessa Bell' surrounded by drifts of pink rain lily (*Habranthus robustus*).

USING COLOR IN THE GARDEN

Every color except for true blue is now found in roses, including mavericks like lavender, purple, green, gray, brown—even black! With such a range at your fingertips, understanding some basic garden color principles will help you design the most elegant garden possible.

Rose colors can be roughly divided into two categories: warm and cool. Warm tones include scarlet, orange, yellow, apricot, buff, peach, and "warm" shades of pink (those with yellow undertones). Cool tones include pure white, blush, lavender, mauve, magenta, burgundy, and "cool" shades of pink (those with lilac undertones).

When designing with roses, the easiest way to avoid color clashes is by keeping warm and cool tones separated, especially when it comes to hot oranges and cool pinks. The blazing orange of 'Chris Evert', for example, would be jarring next to the cool pink of 'Beverly'. But that's not to say that you should avoid mixing roses entirely. To the contrary, exciting gardens can be created by mixing different roses. Here are a few ways to execute that successfully:

For a refreshing splash of cool colors in the garden, mix lavender 'Poseidon' with burgundy fountain grass and crisp white annual vinca.

First, you can juxtapose strong and weak tones within either the warm or cool colors. Dark pink 'Beverly' would look marvelous next to the lighter pink of 'Memorial Day', as both are cool tones.

Second, you can combine roses of similar tone but contrasting architecture. The large, single-stemmed blooms of 'Beverly' next to the small, clustered blooms of 'Lyda Rose' would create a rousing textural contrast with two harmonious shades of pink.

And finally—hearkening back to the benefits of a mixed planting—imagine 'Beverly', 'Memorial Day', and 'Lyda Rose' combined in a bed with other cool-toned plants: burgundy-leaved cordylines, violet dwarf ruellias, soft pink pentas or rain lilies, and perhaps a purple passionflower vine as a vertical accent. Throw in some muted neutrals—muhly grass, variegated pittos-porum, our native scorpiontail flower—and voila! You now have a completely harmonious garden design, with multiple layers of color, texture, biodiversity, native plants, and wildlife attractants.

These same principles apply just as well to warm-toned roses. I'm not a fan of orange flowers in general, but were I to use 'Chris Evert' in a land-scape scheme, some congenial cohorts might be other plants in shades of red, gold, yellow, and bronze: crotons, heliconias, dwarf firebush, Cuban but-tercup—even perhaps an orange geiger, one of South Florida's handsomest native trees, to pick up the orange in 'Chris Evert'. Including a few blue flow-ers—plumbago, salvia, evolvulus—is also particularly effective in balancing out warm-toned roses.

A simple but elegant pairing, 'Princess Charlene de Monaco' shines against a mass of umbrella sedge (*Cyperus alternifolius*) in this North Miami garden.

My last bit of advice where color is concerned is this: learn to love plants with gray or silver foliage. Where roses are concerned, gray-leafed plants work *wonders* for preventing color clashes between disparate tones. If a client really wanted 'Beverly' and 'Chris Evert' in the same bed, I would separate them with some rosemary, Texas sage, false boldo, a sweet almond bush—any splash of gray will soften an otherwise discordant color clash.

ROSES IN CONTAINERS

Container-grown roses have many pluses. Since nematodes aren't an issue in potting soil, you have the option of growing roses even if they're not grafted on 'Fortuniana'. Containerized roses also offer solutions for apartment dwellers, gardeners with mobility problems, or (for people like me) the overly obsessed who need to cram just *one* more rose into their garden somehow.

The biggest drawback to container gardening is watering. Due to South Florida's constant warmth, containerized roses need daily watering, especially in summer. You're also limited to smaller, bushier varieties; large-growing roses will suffer with their roots overly cramped.

Any type of container will do, as long as it is 7 gallons or larger and has drainage holes in place. Many containers, especially clay or ceramic, will be extremely heavy once planted and watered, so stage them in their final location prior to planting. Be sure to use a top-quality potting soil. Aftercare (pruning and fertilizing) will be otherwise similar to that for in-ground roses.

CUTTING ROSES FOR ARRANGEMENTS

While your local florist offers a variety of cut roses, these pale in comparison to the beauty and fragrance of home-grown cut roses. Even the humblest garden roses have a certain magic that their refrigerated cousins at the store never quite capture.

Roses are best cut early in the morning, ideally by 7:00 a.m. or so. Always use sharp secateurs to ensure clean cuts and minimize any damage done to the plant. Try to choose stems that are at least 7" or longer in length; shorter stems may be difficult to arrange. For the longest-lasting arrangement possible, include some buds that are half-open.

'Red Eden's nonstop brilliant crimson flowers are sweetly perfumed on hot days, but less so in cool weather.

The best way to harvest roses is to bring a bucket of lukewarm (not cold) water out into the garden with you. Cut your roses one at a time, immediately plunging them into water as you go. Make an angled cut directly above a growth eye (where a leaf connects to the cane).

When you're ready to arrange your flowers, give each stem a fresh snip with your secateurs and remove any leaves that will end up underwater in the finished arrangement. I like to use a small, sharp knife (a steak knife works well) to shave about an inch of green off the bottom of each stem before arranging them. This ensures maximum water absorption—and a longer vase life—for each flower.

4

100 Roses A to Z

HOW TO USE THE "100 ROSES A TO Z" GUIDE

The guide that follows will introduce you to 100 of the best-performing and beautiful roses for South Florida gardens, with the class and date of introduction (if known) noted after each name.

For each variety described, a list of essential features regarding that rose's growth habits, culture, history, and horticultural applications is included to help you make the best possible choices for your garden. Here's an introduction to those features.

Hybridizer or Discoverer: The person who either bred the variety or discovered it and brought it into cultivation; in some cases, only their surname is known. Occasionally, this person remains unknown entirely.

Culture: How easy or hard each variety is for the average gardener to grow successfully (that is, with a respectable show of flowers on a relatively healthy plant).

Availability: "Wide" indicates varieties carried by at least three or more online retailers; they are often available in local nurseries as well. "Moderate" indicates varieties available in at least one or two online stores and the occasional local nursery. Roses with "limited" availability may be hard to find, typically because they are new releases.

Fragrance: This describes the variety's floral scent.

Average size: The average dimensions you can expect the variety to attain; many can be kept toward the shorter end of this range through judicious pruning.

Disease resistance: The variety's overall disease resistance when planted well and provided adequate light and air circulation.

Rebloom: "Excellent" indicates roses that bloom profusely all year long in South Florida. "Good" varieties will bloom acceptably well throughout the year. Those listed as "fair" tend to have sparse flowering throughout the year.

Garden uses: Suggestions on how each variety would be best utilized in the landscape.

Flowerbeds: individual rosebushes used in mixed plantings with other garden plants.

Cut flowers: varieties good for arrangements.

Groupings: roses that look good in groups of three or more of the same variety.

Specimen: varieties with handsome, symmetrical shrubs that work well as accent plants.

Climber: small or medium climbers useful for trellises, arches, and obelisks; larger climbers best reserved for fences, large arbors, and pergolas.

Containers: compact varieties that can be grown in large pots indefinitely.

Hedge: dense varieties good for creating hedges of various heights.

Own-root: varieties naturally resistant to root-knot nematodes; these need not be grafted on 'Fortuniana' to survive in South Florida.

Pollinators: roses that are attractive to bees and butterflies.

Partial shade: varieties that tolerate (or prefer) partial shade.

Conversation piece: roses with amusing, quirky, or otherwise fascinating tales behind them.

ABOUT FACE

Grandiflora, 2005

I didn't think much of 'About Face' for many years because the flower color was way too strident for my tastes back then. (I say "back then" as if the 2010s are now considered classical antiquity.) But over time, this rose's qualities have grown on me—particularly the bountiful flower production.

The name is instantly fitting the moment you see these blossoms: ochre-yellow petals with a sharply contrasting vermilion-orange reverse. The bicolor effect is especially striking when buds are about one-third open. Mature flowers are rounded to cup-shaped and appear pumpkin orange with darker centers from a distance. The flowers, which give off a delightful green-apple fragrance, are generously produced from forked, upright-facing clusters of shapely, pointed-ovoid buds.

'About Face' forms an upright, narrow plant around 6' tall at maturity. The canes are *extremely* thorny for most of their length—be careful when working around them. The very dark, almost black-green leaves have a reddish tinge and show good disease resistance.

Like many roses in South Florida, 'About Face's flowers will be less double in hot weather, with their stamens displayed prominently then. The reduced petal count renders the blooms more attractive to bees and other pollinators, however—sort of an eco-friendly silver lining to the aesthetic defect.

Hybridizer: Tom Carruth
Culture: Easy
Availability: Wide
Fragrance: Pleasant green apple
Average Size: 6' tall × 4–5' wide
Disease Resistance: Good
Rebloom: Excellent
Garden Uses: Flowerbeds, cut flowers, groupings

ABRAHAM DARBY

Shrub (David Austin), 1985

'Abraham Darby' is one of David Austin's most popular creations from the 1980s, still widely sold today. Named after an English hero of the Industrial Revolution, he packs a big punch with massive, beautifully formed sensuously fragrant blooms.

Though marketed as a shrub, 'Abraham Darby' is really a climber in South Florida—mostly as a result of his vigorous, somewhat floppy growth that gradually arches upward. The glossy, emerald-green foliage is, unfortunately, blackspot-prone, but Abe is so vigorous that the plant will continue to grow and bloom even when infected.

Flowers, either singly or in branched sprays, start out as plump yellow buds smudged with pink. These open up into big, deeply cupped blooms packed with petals like the best antique roses. In cool weather they're a deep, warm pink shaded with gold and apricot toward their base; summer heat lightens them to peachy pink fading to white in the outer petals. Regardless of season, 'Abraham Darby' is powerfully fragrant with a seductive, sweet pineapple aroma.

'Abraham Darby's flowers are so big and heavy that they almost always nod under their own weight on the stems. The best solution is to let Abe grow as a climber on either side of a garden arch. This way, when the heavy flowers inevitably begin to droop, they are already 5' or so off the ground—the perfect height for both viewing and sniffing.

Hybridizer: David Austin
Culture: Somewhat challenging
Availability: Wide
Fragrance: Rich, strong pineapple
Average Size: 8–10' tall × 6–8' wide
Disease Resistance: Fair
Rebloom: Good
Garden Uses: Medium climber, cut flowers

ADAM

Tea, 1838

Generally accepted as the first tea rose ever bred in Europe, it's only fitting that his creators named 'Adam' after the biblical Adam, another first of his kind. Sadly, 'Adam' is rarely grown nowadays—a real shame, as this variety is a crucial part of the rose genetics we enjoy today.

'Adam' is one of the more floppy tea roses and seems to grow best as a climber. Most other teas form bushy, relatively upright shrubs, but 'Adam's canes are loose and lax, reaching 10' or more with proper support. Stems and branches are not overly thorny, a big plus when it comes time for training or maintenance.

Flowers, in loose sprays, start out as pointed dark pink buds. These gently open into nodding, full, deeply cupped flowers of two-tone pink: silvery blush on top, deep rose on the reverse. Flowers are beautifully quartered during mild weather; the outer petals typically reflex and roll their edges back to create pointed tips. The vivid red new growth and dark blue-green mature leaves all harmonize beautifully with the blooms.

'Adam' is one of those heirloom varieties you'll cherish just because of the name as well as its place in rose history. A single plant set off as a prominent vertical accent is all you need to honor this early crusader of modern roses.

Hybridizer: Mons. Adam
Culture: Somewhat challenging
Availability: Moderate
Fragrance: Strong, sweet tea
Average Size: 8–10' tall × 5–8' wide
Disease Resistance: Fair
Rebloom: Good
Garden Uses: Medium climber, cut flowers, own-root,
conversation piece

AGRIPPINA

China, 1832

Despite being one of the more common China roses in commerce today, 'Agrippina' has a history complicated enough to induce headaches in even seasoned rose experts.

First, 'Agrippina' has a dozen aliases in the nursery trade: 'Cramoisi Supérieur', 'Lady Brisbane', 'Queen of Scarlet', 'La Gaufrée', 'Old Bermuda Red', and six or seven others. And because of these many names, several different breeders from the 1800s claimed to have created this rose, including Coquereau, Coquerel (not to be confused with Coquereau), Villoresi, Paillet, and John J. Rule. The date of introduction ranges from 1818 to 1858. And finally, some rosarians insist that the reason for this mess of names, breeders, and dates is because multiple different roses are now called 'Agrippina'. Multiple different roses with the same name? Pass the ibuprofen.

Fortunately, you don't have to be a historian to enjoy 'Agrippina'. Flowering all year long in South Florida, small blossoms of bright ruby-scarlet are held in branched terminal clusters. Inner petals are often a lighter shade of red, and one or two of the main petals are streaked with white. Flowers sometimes nod horizontally on their slender pedicels. The dense, twiggy shrub reaches around 8' tall and wide at maturity but can be kept smaller via pruning.

This is a very low-maintenance rose for South Florida, well adapted to our humid heat and virtually immune to blackspot. I frequently see 'Agrippina' as an unlabeled, own-root rose in various wholesale nurseries here. Whether or not these are the "real" 'Agrippina' is anyone's guess, but we can take solace in the fact that even the experts can't agree on what (or who or when).

Hybridizer: Unknown
Culture: Easy
Availability: Wide
Fragrance: Light, peppery
Average Size: 4–8' tall × 4–8' wide
Disease Resistance: Excellent
Rebloom: Excellent
Garden Uses: Flowerbeds, cut flowers, groupings, hedge, own-root

ARCHDUKE CHARLES

China, 1825

Modern roses that change color with exposure to sunlight are a delight to today's gardeners, and all of these chameleons can be traced back to the China roses. *Rosa chinensis* is the source of the gene that allows for rose petals to "suntan," and there is no more perfect exemplar of this than 'Archduke Charles.'

A color sport of the famous China 'Old Blush', 'Archduke Charles' flowers in big flushes throughout the year, and the color display is nothing short of stunning. Flowers start out as upright sprays of dark pink, hybrid tea-shaped buds. These open into full, shapely flowers done up in light pink and lilac, with lipstick red on the outer petals. The red tones spread as the flowers age, so that they appear totally red by their third day. A mature shrub is a rainbow of reds and pinks in the garden, exhaling a light, sweet scent all the while.

'Archduke Charles' forms a bushy plant to around 5' tall and wide at maturity, though definitely capable of larger dimensions. Large, wavy-textured leaflets are a polished blue green and have superb disease resistance.

This rose deserves much wider use in South Florida: it is readily available, grows well as an own-root plant, and perfectly tackles our humid heat. If you want to dress up your 'Archduke Charles' even more, create a pink and purple "eleganza extravaganza" by pairing it with pink and lavender annual vinca (*Catharanthus*) and a few purple-leaved colocasias.

Hybridizer: Jean Laffay
Culture: Easy
Availability: Wide
Fragrance: Light, sweet, peppery
Average Size: 5' tall × 5' wide
Disease Resistance: Excellent
Rebloom: Excellent
Garden Uses: Flowerbeds, cut flowers, groupings, hedge, own-root

BEAUTÉ INCONSTANTE

Tea, 1887

Although the French name translates as "fickle beauty," the only thing fickle about 'Beauté Inconstante' is the color. Everything else is as dependable as the daily sunrise.

One of the lesser-known (and lesser-grown) tea roses, 'Beauté Inconstante' forms a somewhat open mass of ascending canes lined with the sparse but painfully hooked thorns typical of tea roses. The foliage is remarkably modern looking: large, semiglossy leaflets of a lush, dark blue green, loosely arranged up and down the canes.

Although the base color is a warm deep pink, this changes considerably based on heat and sunlight intensity, with shades of orange, yellow, brick red, and pale apricot blended in like a parfait off and on throughout the year. While summer blooms are a little small, winter flowers are spectacularly large (5" or more across) with attractive rhomboid-shaped petals creating an interesting pentagon outline. The long-stemmed, richly perfumed flowers are excellent for cutting.

'Beauté Inconstante' is a superb rose here, perfectly adapted to our growing conditions and showcasing an extremely unique floral shape and color. Don't let the name throw you off; this rose's performance is most definitely constant and wonderful. Plant 'Beauté Inconstante' in groupings of three for the best floral display possible.

Hybridizer: Joseph Pernet-Ducher
Culture: Easy
Availability: Wide
Fragrance: Strong, sweet tea
Average Size: 5–6' tall × 5–6' wide
Disease Resistance: Excellent
Rebloom: Excellent
Garden Uses: Flowerbeds, cut flowers, groupings, own-root

BELINDA'S DREAM / BELINDA'S BLUSH

Shrub, 1992 ('Belinda's Dream') and 2014 ('Belinda's Blush')

I once joked that if you can't grow 'Belinda's Dream', you should give up gardening and find a new hobby. Truly, I can't overemphasize how easy, low-maintenance—really, how unbreakable—this rose is. An established plant will tolerate substantial neglect while one given lots of TLC will make you look like an expert rose grower to the neighbors.

Although classed as a shrub rose, 'Belinda's Dream' produces perfect hybrid tea-shaped flowers that instantly appeal to gardeners seeking a florist-style rose. Large oval buds gently open up into very full blooms of clear, soft carnation pink. Flowers can appear either single stemmed or in small sprays; along with their sweet raspberry fragrance and long vase life, they're wonderful for cutting.

The handsome, light green, serrated leaflets are completely disease-free all year long. The shrub itself is upright and rounded in outline, with symmetrical branching that works equally well as a specimen or in groupings.

A pale sport, 'Belinda's Blush', was introduced in 2014. Differing only in color, 'Belinda's Blush' features petals of pearlescent blush pink with a warm glow in their centers. The tips of the petals are kissed with a faint trace of the darker pink of 'Belinda's Dream'—a gentle nod of respect to the original.

The two Belindas complement each other perfectly colorwise; if your garden allows, plant them next to each other in the same bed. Blue or violet flowers would look stunning in combination—angelonias, salvias, or blue plumbagos are just a few of the many possibilities.

Hybridizers: Dr. Robert Basye ('Belinda's Dream'); Mike Shoup
    ('Belinda's Blush')
Culture: Easy
Availability: Wide
Fragrance: Strong raspberry
Average Size: 5–6' tall × 4–5' wide
Disease Resistance: Excellent
Rebloom: Excellent
Garden Uses: Flowerbeds, cut flowers, groupings, specimen, hedge,
    Earth-Kind® ('Belinda's Dream')

BERMUDA'S KATHLEEN

China, 1956

A carefree shrub almost never out of bloom is invaluable for "general land-scaping"—industry code for low-maintenance garden plants in either residential or commercial settings. 'Bermuda's Kathleen' is one such rose. One of my hopes for the future is to see this variety used in more commercial landscapes, especially in place of the much-overused (and usually ratty-looking) 'Knock Out' roses.

A seedling of the famous old China 'Mutabilis', 'Bermuda's Kathleen' features similarly single-petaled, open flowers that are great for pollinators. The 2" blooms are pale pink at first but quickly darken to taffy pink and finally finish up as a luminous raspberry red before shattering. Individual flowers present a row of silky, rounded, bilobed petals surrounding an attractive clump of prominent yellow stamens, usually with a few random petaloids (stamens converted into miniature petals) for good measure.

Flowers are carried in large, upward-pointing trusses of 20 or more tiny, elegantly pointed buds. Stop deadheading in late summer, and the branched clusters will form handsome reddish-orange hips that make awesome fall arrangements.

'Bermuda's Kathleen' forms a dense, billowing shrub usually wider than tall. The glossy, pointed leaves exhibit great disease resistance. This rose makes a wonderful everblooming shrub for mass plantings, equally at home in a suburban backyard or a public plaza—the beautiful kaleidoscope of pinks and reds is dazzling no matter the context.

Hybridizer: Unknown
Culture: Easy
Availability: Wide
Fragrance: Light to none
Average Size: 4–6' tall × 5–7' wide
Disease Resistance: Excellent
Rebloom: Excellent
Garden Uses: Flowerbeds, groupings, hedge, own-root, pollinators

BEVERLY®

Hybrid Tea, 2007

It's always good when my only complaint about a rose is that the flower color can be difficult to place in the landscape. Such is the case with 'Beverly', another rock star from the House of Kordes in Germany. Kordes roses are given rigorous field testing to ensure superb disease resistance, and 'Beverly' is no exception: the large, dark green leaves are among the healthiest of any hybrid tea I've ever trialed.

Flowers are produced one per stem. Big, round, dark pink buds with handsome reddish sepals become large, very full flowers of a cool, dark candy pink fading to white near the base. Half-opened blooms have the high-centered "teacup" shape iconic of most hybrid teas while mature flowers flatten out considerably and develop an antique rose look—a charming transformation overall. A strong, spicy old-rose perfume is the perfect finishing touch.

'Beverly' can be kept around 5' tall but often throws out a vigorous shoot to 7' or more, so plan for a spot near the back of a planting bed. The upper stems have a purplish tint that mingles well with the foliage and flower colors.

"Cool" pink roses like 'Beverly' tend to clash jarringly with yellows, oranges, and warm peachy pinks but look great when paired with blue or violet flowers as well as plants with gray or purple foliage. For a cool and crisp color combination, try 'Beverly' against a backdrop of burgundy Jamaica crotons or silver Texas sage (*Leucophyllum frutescens*) and a foreground planting of dwarf 'Katie Blue' ruellias.

Hybridizer: Wilhelm Kordes
Culture: Easy
Availability: Wide
Fragrance: Strong old rose
Average Size: 5–6' tall × 4' wide
Disease Resistance: Excellent
Rebloom: Excellent
Garden Uses: Flowerbeds, cut flowers, groupings

BLACK BACCARA

Hybrid Tea, 2000

I deleted and re-added 'Black Baccara' from this compendium about ten times before finally giving in. Healthwise, this is *not* one of the best roses for South Florida—it's both a fussy grower and a disease magnet, with my lone trial plant getting shovel-pruned shortly after the evaluation period was over.

But it's hard to ignore a blooming specimen of 'Black Baccara'—especially at a nursery with one's credit card nearby. The petals are the sultriest, most sensuous blackish-red color imaginable. Unopened buds are sometimes pure black, slowly spiraling open into truly immaculate florist-style roses. (Fun fact: 'Black Baccara' is an actual floral industry rose, commonly grown in cut-flower farms worldwide!)

Although a hybrid tea in lineage, 'Black Baccara' usually produces sprays of flowers like a grandiflora; not at all a bad thing in my book. The foliage is lovely—gently undulate leaflets of glossy jade green—but *very* disease-prone, with sickly canes often suffering considerable dieback. When healthy and happy, this cultivar makes an upright, viciously thorny, rather ungainly shrub to around 6' tall.

Roses like 'Black Baccara' that feature stunning flowers atop frail or awkward shrubs are best reserved for a cutting garden. Since the peak bloom in South Florida almost always coincides with Valentine's Day, capitalize on this by clipping a single, flawless flower for someone special on February 14th.

Hybridizer: Jacques Mouchotte
Culture: Somewhat challenging
Availability: Moderate
Fragrance: None
Average Size: 6–7' tall × 4–5' wide
Disease Resistance: Poor
Rebloom: Good
Garden Uses: Cut flowers, conversation piece

BRIAN MICHAEL

Shrub, 2019

In South Florida, most roses' colors tend to be deeper in winter and lighter in summer. But with white roses like 'Brian Michael', our climate seems to have an inverse effect: they are pure white in the cool of winter but gain a noticeable yellow blush in heat of summer. Some gardeners dislike this color "impurity," but I find that the lemony summertime tones give each flower a magical luminescence. Bring on the heat!

'Brian Michael' forms an upright, vase-shaped shrub composed of gracefully ascending canes to around 6' tall with semiweeping side branches. New growth is a cheerful bright green that darkens with maturity. Disease resistance has been strong in my evaluations.

Flowers are typically produced in sprays of three or four. Pointed, yellowish buds with lime-green sepals open into full, rounded, heartbreakingly old-fashioned blossoms up to 4" across with reflexed guard petals. A large button eye anchors the center of each blossom like an overstuffed ottoman in a living room. The fragrance is a delicious, strong mix of lemony old rose and myrrh.

'Brian Michael' is truly ceaseless in flower production; along with 'Faith Whittlesey', this is one of the heaviest-blooming white roses I've ever grown. You'll definitely want to cut blooms for the house; a single spray is enough to perfume a room. This rose was named for my partner, Brian Michael Bocci.

Discoverer: Geoff Coolidge
Culture: Easy
Availability: Limited
Fragrance: Outstanding old rose/myrrh blend
Average Size: 5–6' tall × 4–5' wide
Disease Resistance: Good
Rebloom: Excellent
Garden Uses: Flowerbeds, cut flowers, groupings

CARNATION

China, date unknown

Sometimes you just want a *fun* rose to put in your garden—and 'Carnation' is nothing if not fun!

One look at the flowers and you'll instantly understand the name. The deeply cupped, almost cylindrical blooms have crimped and fringed petal margins with white tracing along the tips, closely resembling the blooms of a traditional carnation (*Dianthus caryophyllus*). The flowers, which are usually deep pink, can darken to almost lilac in cool weather—a blessing for those who enjoy purple-toned roses. Pointed buds come in big branching sprays, with mature shrubs producing some truly breathtaking flower flushes.

Unusual for a China, 'Carnation' forms a fastigiate shrub taller than wide, similar in habit to 'Vincent Godsiff' but larger. The attractive slate-green foliage is not as blackspot resistant as other China roses, but in my Cape Coral garden, fallen leaves are so quickly replaced that I never bother to spray.

'Carnation' is one of several "Bermuda Mystery" roses, unheard of except as a garden plant in Bermuda until a sample was collected and propagated by famous Florida rosarian Dr. Malcolm Manners in 1988. After a mandatory two-year federal quarantine and evaluation period, 'Carnation' was deemed safe for commercial release and quickly spread to other nurseries around the United States.

Virtually all "Bermuda Mystery" roses currently grown in America can be traced back to the efforts of Dr. Manners—classic proof that one person can, indeed, make a difference.

Discoverer: Bermuda Rose Society
Culture: Easy
Availability: Moderate
Fragrance: Light
Average Size: 5–7' tall × 4–5' wide
Disease Resistance: Good
Rebloom: Excellent
Garden Uses: Flowerbeds, cut flowers, groupings, own-root, conversation piece

CHRIS EVERT

Hybrid Tea, 1997

Orange roses seldom make it into my various gardens, as I openly admit to preferring pink and burgundy roses. But in South Florida, it's really hard not to like 'Chris Evert'—the tropical citrus hues just feel so "right" here. This cultivar was named for the top-ranked tennis player who was born in Fort Lauderdale and currently resides in Boca Raton, so the connection to South Florida is more than apropos.

'Chris Evert' is a big rose with respect to the Four Fs: form, foliage, flower, and fragrance. Growthwise, expect thick, thorny canes creating a tall, vertical shrub loosely draped in large, dark green, semiglossy leaves. The bulky-yet-shapely blooms, fiery tangerine orange smudged with red and gold, emerge from long, spiraled buds of the same colors. New growth is plum purple—always attractive when contrasted with orange flowers of any kind—and the fragrance is a strong, fruity aroma that will knock your socks off.

The bright orange of 'Chris Evert' associates effortlessly with most of our other tropical garden fare. For a flashy garden scheme that really says "South Florida," try a group of three in the center of a bed, with a backdrop of 'Yellow Mammy' or 'Sloppy Painter' crotons, some red shrimp plants, a few 'Little Harv' aechmeas, and an edging of dwarf purple alternanthera.

Hybridizer: Tom Carruth
Culture: Easy
Availability: Wide
Fragrance: Powerful, fruity
Average Size: 6' tall × 4–5' wide
Disease Resistance: Good
Rebloom: Excellent
Garden Uses: Flowerbeds, cut flowers, groupings

CHRYSLER IMPERIAL

Hybrid Tea, 1952

Red hybrid teas will always be a part of gardens. They are to gardens what the panda bear is to China: an iconic ambassador, a universal symbol of that world. 'Chrysler Imperial' is an older red but is still widely grown today, largely due to its heavy perfume and rich coloration.

'Chrysler Imperial' forms more of a rounded, spreading plant than most other hybrid teas, which tend to be stiffly upright. New growth is reddish bronze, maturing to dull matte green. The large, ovoid, dark red buds spiral open into large, beautifully shaped florists' roses of rich velvety crimson. As the flowers age, the color turns into more of a cherry red with magenta and purplish lowlights. They are sumptuously perfumed with a powerful damask fragrance all the while.

This rose does especially well in South Florida; the blooms open best in hot weather but may ball and turn brown if the weather is both cool and damp—which is rarely a problem for us here as our cool season is also our dry season.

This variety was named for the famous luxury car originally developed and released by Chrysler Automobiles in 1926; it remained Chrysler's highest-priced model for most of the company's history. Alongside corporate rivals Cadillac and Lincoln, the Chrysler Imperial reigned as one of America's top cars for much of the 1930s, '40s, and '50s. Sales began to decline in the late 1960s, and the model was officially canceled in 2006.

Hybridizer: Dr. Walter E. Lammerts
Culture: Easy
Availability: Wide
Fragrance: Outstanding damask
Average Size: 4' tall × 4–5' wide
Disease Resistance: Fair
Rebloom: Good
Garden Uses: Flowerbeds, cut flowers, groupings

CIEN HOJAS

Portland or Bourbon, date unknown

No one rose has caused me so much ID frustration than 'Cien Hojas'. Nobody really knows what class it belongs to—the Bourbons? The Portlands? Something else? This variety came to me from a gardening friend in Puerto Rico, who posted it for sale on Facebook. Reasoning that if this rose thrived in Puerto Rico, it would probably do well in South Florida too, I bought three.

'Cien Hojas' makes a rounded little shrub to about 4' tall and wide. The green canes have sharp, hooked thorns arranged spirally along their length. Leaflets are soft gray green and handsomely serrated; they come right up to the base of the pedicels, like the foliage of most Portland roses.

Small clusters of pointed, reddish-pink buds with feathery sepals open up into rose-pink, loosely double, flat-cupped flowers with gently scalloped tips. Petals take on pale lilac tones as they age. Blooms emit a tangy damask fragrance, another calling card of many of the Portlands as well as some Bourbons. Rebloom is weak on young plants but improves as they mature.

The seller said that he only knew this rose as 'Cien Hojas' (Spanish for "hundred leaves") and that it was a fairly common garden plant in Puerto Rico. I have not found a rose by this name in any rose database search, and my attempts to ID this rose based on photos have also been fruitless.

'Cien Hojas' is the Spanish translation of "centifolia," but true centifolias are all strictly once-blooming roses that need cold weather to flower. As 'Cien Hojas' is both heat tolerant and reblooming, it definitely isn't a true centifolia rose—hence the additional confusion. The real identity of this rose may be a mystery forever.

Hybridizer: Unknown
Culture: Easy
Availability: Limited
Fragrance: Strong damask
Average Size: 4–5' tall × 4–5' wide
Disease Resistance: Good
Rebloom: Good
Garden Uses: Flowerbeds, cut flowers, groupings, own-root,
    conversation piece

CLEMENTINA CARBONIERI

Tea, 1913

The tea roses have a reputation for a color range limited to soft pastels. For those who want something that's definitely *not* pastel, 'Clementina Carbonieri' is the way to go. Sizzling like neon signs in the garden, these flowers rival the gaudiest of modern roses, but on a heathy, low-maintenance plant.

'Clementina Carbonieri' is usually described as "leaning on its elbows," a poetic way of saying that the plant has a sprawling, wider-than-tall growth habit. New growth is burgundy and matures to rich green with a semiglossy sheen; individual leaflets curl slightly downward. Like most other tea roses in South Florida, disease resistance is excellent.

Flowers are small (2–3") but exceptionally brilliant. The base color is salmon pink blended with yellow, but neon orange and hot fuchsia are splashed around liberally. The outer petals occasionally show markings of deep magenta violet, adding to the color carnival. The fluffy, pompon-shaped flowers are blessed with a wonderful tea fragrance and are sometimes quartered in cool weather.

I've grown 'Clementina Carbonieri' in all my various South Florida gardens, and the performance is always Oscar worthy—this cultivar simply loves our humid heat. Add to that good online availability, and you have a fabulous little rose packing a great big punch.

Hybridizer: Massamiliano Lodi
Culture: Easy
Availability: Wide
Fragrance: Strong sweet tea/fruit blend
Average Size: 3–4' tall × 4–5' wide
Disease Resistance: Good
Rebloom: Excellent
Garden Uses: Flowerbeds, cut flowers, groupings, own-root

CLOTILDE SOUPERT

Polyantha, 1888

Although summer blooms are frequently spoiled by balling, 'Clotilde Soupert' is nonetheless an excellent South Florida rose. This is easily one of the most blackspot-resistant old roses I've ever grown—almost as good as 'Louis-Philippe'—and cool season flowers generally have none of the balling issue prevalent in summertime. For me, a few months of spoiled flowers is totally worth the "sou-perb" winter and spring display. And, let's be honest: few South Floridians want to be gardening in August anyway.

Branched sprays of plump, greenish-pink buds turn into 3", extremely full rosettes jam-packed with petals (up to 100 per flower!) in handsome symmetry. They are frosty white with pink blushing in their centers, excellent when placed against a dark green hedge or a dark-toned house or wall. The fragrance is a refreshingly sharp blend of tea and bell peppers, similar to the scent of 'Louis-Phillipe' but far sweeter and less acidic.

'Clotilde Soupert' comes in two forms: as a shrub to around 4' tall with a wider spread and as a climbing sport that can reach 15' or more with proper support. Both feature handsome light green foliage and reddish stems lined with hooked thorns. While the shrub form is great for containers and small spaces, I prefer the climbing version. Cascading over a fence, arch, or pergola, the romantic antique-shaped blooms look like something straight out of *Romeo and Juliet*.

Hybridizer: Soupert & Notting
Culture: Easy
Availability: Wide
Fragrance: Excellent sweet tea/pepper blend
Average Size: Varies by form
Disease Resistance: Excellent
Bloom Frequency: Good
Garden Uses: Flowerbeds, cut flowers, groupings, Earth-Kind, own-root, containers (bush form), large climber (climbing form)

CORNELIA

Shrub (Hybrid Musk), 1925

'Cornelia' is another excellent climber for South Florida. The snaking, sinuous canes and fountain-like habit are easy to train vertically, and the pendant flower trusses look incredible when dangling overhead. 'Cornelia' also does well as a freestanding shrub—just make sure you give the plant plenty of space to flop around, as it dislikes heavy pruning.

Rounded, dark pink buds with stubby sepals open up into loosely double, sweetly fragrant cups of warm salmon pink with prominent stamens. Each bloom is too heavy for its slender stalk, resulting in a stunningly romantic weeping effect. The ropey canes are mostly thornless, great for use near patios or pathways.

A typical hybrid musk, 'Cornelia' is shrouded in healthy leaves composed of seven slender, pointed leaflets. The flowers, which come in flushes throughout the year, are arranged along the stems in a fishbone pattern.

Like 'Penelope', 'Cornelia' is another rose named after a legendary woman of strong character. Born around 190 BCE, Cornelia Africana was the daughter of Scipio Africanus, one of the most brilliant military strategists in ancient Rome. Over the course of her life, Cornelia became a paragon to Roman women. Despite her wealth and power, she was by all accounts a kind and modest woman who wore simple clothes—"My children are my jewels," she replied when asked why she never wore jewelry—and devoted her life to studying language, literature, art, and politics.

Hybridizer: Rev. Joseph Hardwick Pemberton
Culture: Easy
Availability: Wide
Fragrance: Strong musk/tea blend
Average Size: 8–20' tall × 8–15' wide
Disease Resistance: Good
Rebloom: Good
Garden Uses: Large climber, cut flowers, specimen, own-root, partial
    shade, conversation piece

CRÉPUSCULE

Tea-Noisette, 1904

The tea-Noisettes are one of the most elegant subclasses of roses ever created, with head-to-toe good looks. Many modern roses, especially the hybrid teas, have gorgeous blooms on top of ugly shrubs. Not so with the tea-Noisettes: every inch of their anatomy radiates class and beauty.

'Crépuscule' is one such delight, always at the top of my list for a climber to use on a pergola or other large structure. The canes are a study in simple beauty: light green maturing to luscious mahogany brown and mostly thornless along their length. Pointed, dark green leaflets droop down from the canes to create a weeping effect.

Flowers, in bunches of three to five, begin as reddish-orange buds that open into small, loose, open flowers of soft peachy orange with blush-apricot highlights. Just like the leaves, 'Crépscule's flowers typically hang down in a cascade of petals. A sweet aroma of tea rose and pepper emanates from the blossoms.

Mature tea-Noisettes generally have an explosive fall and spring flush in South Florida with sparser scatterings of blooms in between. They make great "snowbird" roses for this reason, giving a grand floral display just as frost-dreading northerners are returning for the winter and, again, right before they leave for the summer.

Hybridizer: Francis Dubreuil
Culture: Easy
Availability: Moderate
Fragrance: Strong pepper/tea blend
Average Size: 15–20' tall × 8–15' wide
Disease Resistance: Excellent
Rebloom: Good
Garden Uses: Large climber, cut flowers, pollinators, light shade, own-root

CYD'S COMPASSION

Tea, 2013

This dainty darling is one of several releases from Florida hybridizer Allen Whitcomb, who made great efforts to produce beautiful garden roses that prosper in our humid heat. 'Cyd's Compassion' is one of his best creations, merging a unique blossom onto a truly unstoppable flower factory of a shrub.

Upright sprays of lipstick-pink buds open up into 2–3", loosely double, cupped to deeply globular flowers. Their color varies from a uniform soft pink to a lovely bicolored white and pink parfait; bicolored blooms seem to occur mostly in hot weather, when the petal count is fewer.

A big part of this variety's appeal lies in its petite proportions. Many tea roses become large shrubs in South Florida, but 'Cyd's Compassion' stays reliably under 4' tall without any drastic pruning—perfect for small spaces and containers. All of Cyd's parts are correspondingly small in scale, from the twiggy canes, to the small blue-green leaves, to the wee blooms with their light perfume.

'Cyd's Compassion' has proven to be one of my heaviest bloomers, frequently covered in flushes of 40 or more buds at a time. The variety was named for Cydney Wade, a family friend of Whitcomb and a fellow rose grower herself.

Hybridizer: Allen Whitcomb
Culture: Easy
Availability: Limited
Fragrance: Light, sweet
Average Size: 3–4' tall × 3–4' wide
Disease Resistance: Excellent
Rebloom: Excellent
Garden Uses: Flowerbeds, cut flowers, groupings, own-root, containers

DAMES DE CHENONCEAU®

Floribunda, 2002

Although classed as a floribunda, 'Dames de Chenonceau' throws out long, thorny canes to around 8' or so in South Florida. This makes for a splendid small climber in our area; with good training, the lateral buds explode with flowering shoots like a fountain of flowers.

Small clusters of plump ovoid buds are vivid fuchsia at first. These open into large, full, antique-looking blooms of warm pink with deeper shading in their centers. The fragrance is divine—a strong blend of anise, myrrh, and fruit—and the flowers are wonderfully long lasting when cut. Semiglossy leaves are bright forest green with each leaflet folded upward along its midrib.

This rose commemorates the "Ladies of Chenonceau," a group of famous women who lived in Chateau de Chenonceau, one of the most historically significant buildings in France. Built in 1522, Chenonceau has been home to such notables as Diane de Poitiers (mistress to King Francis I), Catherine de Medici (queen to Henry II), Louise de Lorraine (queen to Henry III), and—perhaps most famously—Louise Dupin, a philanthropist and socialite in the 1700s who attracted so many artists, writers, and philosophers to Chenonceau that it became a hub of the French Enlightenment. Voltaire, Montesquieu, and Rousseau, among others, all gathered by Dupin's side at Chenonceau at one time or another.

It is only fitting that a rose exuding such antique charm was chosen to honor this chateau and its famous women. I can easily imagine Louise Dupin arranging similar roses in her salon as the great minds of France prepared to gather there on some warm summer evening, the air growing heavy with both fragrance and philosophy.

Hybridizer: Georges Delbard
Culture: Easy
Availability: Moderate
Fragrance: Strong, spicy anise/citrus mix
Average Size: 8–10' tall × 6' wide
Disease Resistance: Good
Rebloom: Excellent
Garden Uses: Small climber, cut flowers, groupings, conversation piece

DARCEY BUSSELL

Shrub (David Austin), 2005

'Darcey Bussell' is one of the more reliably low-growing English roses for South Florida—great for us, as even "compact" varieties frequently grow huge here because of our year-round heat. Not so for Miss Bussell: after four years in my garden, my plants have never exceeded 4' tall.

This cultivar serves old rose realness like it's Thanksgiving dinner. Terminal clusters of plump, bull-nosed buds festooned with ornate sepals erupt into large, very full rosettes of deep burgundy highlighted with magenta. The wonderfully intricate, swirling petal formation is like something you'd see painted onto an antique porcelain plate. The aroma is a rich and fruity old rose medley, similar to 'Munstead Wood' but not as strong.

'Darcey Bussell' forms a rounded shrub with sprightly, relatively smooth canes decked out in the softest dark green foliage imaginable. Each rounded leaflet has a beautifully serrated reddish-brown margin. Disease resistance is only moderate, however.

Born in London in 1969, Dame Darcey Andrea Bussell (née Crittle) performed for over 20 years with the Royal Ballet, the largest ballet company in Great Britain and one of the most famous worldwide. Since formally retiring in 2007, Darcey has devoted much of her time and financial resources toward various medical charities and dance associations throughout the United Kingdom and Australia.

Hybridizer: David Austin
Culture: Easy
Availability: Moderate
Fragrance: Rich, fruity old rose
Average Size: 4' tall × 4' wide
Disease Resistance: Good
Rebloom: Excellent
Garden Uses: Flowerbeds, cut flowers, groupings, containers

DOUBLE DELIGHT

Hybrid Tea, 1976

The legend of 'Double Delight'—one of the most famous roses ever—is an incredible rags-to-riches story. Despite becoming one of the most popular roses around the world, winning countless awards, and being among a mere handful of cultivars inducted into the Rose Hall of Fame, the original 'Double Delight' seedling plant was actually almost put in the trash.

The breeder, John Sheldon, thought that 'Double Delight' was just another generic white rose at first. But when the original plant was taken outdoors for disposal, the petal tips turned vivid cherry red—like a gorgeous strawberry-vanilla parfait. The color change was brought about by ultraviolet rays, blocked by the glass of most greenhouses—which is why the greenhouse seedling of 'Double Delight' was thought to be just another unremarkable white rose. This one singular trait saved this rose from the garbage dump and gave its career a 180-degree turnaround.

In South Florida, 'Double Delight' forms a spreading shrub with glossy foliage prone to blackspot without treatment. The strawberries-and-cream color effect is especially stunning on the half-open, urn-shaped flowers, which give off a powerfully spicy perfume—perhaps 'Triple Delight' would more accurately describe this rose.

Back in the early twentieth century, the genes responsible for "suntanning" were viewed as an unpredictable liability. It was only when roses like 'Double Delight' were met with a warm reception (and open wallets) by the gardening public that color-changing roses were explored in earnest by breeders. As one of the early pioneers of this new horizon for roses, 'Double Delight' is a Cinderella story worth repeating time and again.

Hybridizer: John Sheldon
Culture: Easy
Availability: Wide
Fragrance: Sharp citrus/jasmine blend
Average Size: 4–5' tall × 4' wide
Disease Resistance: Fair
Rebloom: Good
Garden Uses: Flowerbeds, cut flowers, groupings, conversation piece

DUCHER

China, 1869

Pronounced "doo-SHAY," this little rose has a lot to offer. Like most Chinas, 'Ducher' is virtually immune to blackspot and laughs in the face of oppressive heat. This variety also has the distinction of being the only white China rose currently in commerce—and who doesn't enjoy bragging about having the only one of something?

'Ducher' forms a low, mounding shrub around 4' tall and wide, smaller than many other Chinas. New growth is a handsome bright red; combined with the pure white flowers and rich green mature leaves, the colors remind me of the Italian flag.

Blooms are produced endlessly throughout the year; they can be single stemmed or in branched sprays. Lime-green buds with ornate sepals unfold into full, sweetly fragrant, cupped flowers of impressive clarity. Older flowers take on a flattened appearance, and the petal edges roll back into pointed tips—a signature look of many Chinas. Freshly shattered flowers give a charming "snowdrift" effect beneath the plant. Some growers claim that the blooms will sunburn in hot weather, but I personally have never observed this.

Claude Ducher (1820–1874) was a French nurseryman and one of the most respected rose breeders in Europe during the 1800s. Beginning his business in 1835, he bred over 90 different varieties during his lifetime, many of which are still grown today. Kudos to him for picking a fantastic selection to bestow the family name upon.

Hybridizer: Claude Ducher
Culture: Easy
Availability: Wide
Fragrance: Strong, sweet honeysuckle
Average Size: 3–4' tall × 4' wide
Disease Resistance: Excellent
Rebloom: Excellent
Garden Uses: Flowerbeds, cut flowers, groupings, containers, Earth-Kind®, own-root, conversation piece

DUCHESSE DE BRABANT

Tea, 1857

This beauty from the mid-1800s was one of the first Earth-Kind roses chosen by Texas A&M University. Selected varieties go through eight years of extensive field testing to prove their mettle. Considering I've had other varieties perish within eight *months,* we can suffice to say that 'Duchesse de Brabant' should be first on any South Floridian's list of roses to buy. This one is titanium.

'Duchesse de Brabant' (pronounced "BRAY-bundt") forms an attractive, haystack-shaped shrub whose symmetry works equally well as a stand-alone specimen, in groupings, or as a lovely, everblooming hedge. Thorns sparsely dot the canes but are large and painful enough to serve well as a barrier plant. The olive-green foliage has flawless disease resistance.

Flowers, usually in branched, open sprays, start out as pointed dark pink buds. These become moderately full, cup-shaped blossoms of soft pink, sometimes with peach shading. The great rose curator Clair Martin described the perfume as a delicate blend of apricots and allspice, and I wholeheartedly agree; it's one of the most unique rose fragrances I've ever experienced.

An antiquated criticism of tea roses is that their flowers often nod because of weak "necks" right below the calyx. This is true for many teas including 'Duchesse de Brabant', but I view the nodding effect as a positive. A mature plant covered in horizontally facing flowers has a curiously animated feel, almost as if the flowers have turned to greet you. I wouldn't have my Duchesse any other way.

Hybridizer: Pierre Bernède
Culture: Easy
Availability: Wide
Fragrance: Strong allspice/apricot blend
Average Size: 5–7' tall × 5–6' wide
Disease Resistance: Excellent
Rebloom: Excellent
Garden Uses: Flowerbeds, cut flowers, groupings, hedge, specimen,
    Earth-Kind®, own-root, pollinators

EASY DOES IT

Floribunda, 2010

Orange lovers, take note: 'Easy Does It' is definitely one to put in your garden. I'm not a huge fan of orange flowers in general, but this rose is so floriferous and carefree that I could easily see designing a whole garden around just this one variety. This rose *really* does its name justice.

'Easy Does It' is an unrelenting blooming machine at maturity, pumping out endless flushes of large, ruffled, mango-colored blooms kissed with salmon and hot pink in the outer petals. The pinkish tones increase as the flowers age. Petals are distinctively notched into several rounded lobes, making them seem almost artificial at first. The tapered buds come either single stemmed or in clusters.

A typical floribunda, 'Easy Does It' forms a vase-shaped, upright, thorny shrub. The glossy, vivid green foliage has excellent disease resistance, with rose gardeners all over the world applauding this as one of the best floribundas healthwise. The shiny leaves are reminiscent of 'Julia Child'—another excellent, everblooming floribunda here. In fact, these two roses' colors would look wonderful together, evoking all the warmth of summer in a single flowerbed.

Hybridizer: Harkness & Company
Culture: Easy
Availability: Wide
Fragrance: Light, fruity
Average Size: 4–5' tall × 4–5' wide
Disease Resistance: Good
Rebloom: Excellent
Garden Uses: Flowerbeds, cut flowers, groupings

EMMIE GRAY

China, date unknown

'Emmie Gray' is a great rose for partial shade positions. I've seen specimens of this variety thriving in the bright afternoon shade on the east side of a house or under the high dappled shade of a mature live oak.

That's not to say that this is a stunning rose. The 2″ flowers are charming, but they are never produced in big flushes at any one time. You're more likely to encounter them peeking out like stars amid the foliage. Long, pointed buds open up into deep watermelon-pink, bowl-shaped blossoms that quickly darken to luminescent crimson. A white splotch in the center of each flower is mostly obscured by the golden stamens. Like most single roses, bees find the blooms irresistible.

The shrub itself is unusually upright and narrow for a China rose, similar to 'Carnation' and 'Vincent Godsiff'. Narrow, pointed, dark green leaflets adorn twiggy stems dotted here and there with sharp, hooked thorns.

Another "Bermuda Mystery" rose, this variety was named for its finder, a beloved teacher who taught at the Bermuda High School for Girls for over 30 years. Ms. Emmie Gray reportedly gave many cuttings of this rose to local garden club members over the years, cementing its reputation as a popular garden plant on the island.

Discoverer: Emmie Gray
Culture: Easy
Availability: Moderate
Fragrance: Light
Average Size: 5–7' tall × 3–6' wide
Disease Resistance: Excellent
Rebloom: Fair
Garden Uses: Flowerbeds, groupings, own-root, pollinators, partial shade

ETOILE DE LYON

Tea, 1881

If 'Etoile de Lyon' never flowered, it would be worth growing for the foliage alone. The tea roses generally have extremely handsome leaves, but 'Etoile de Lyon' takes that concept of beautiful greenery to the next level.

Also called 'Bermuda's Anna Olivier', this cultivar forms a dome-like mass of thorny canes to around 5' tall with a wider spread. Elegant buds with long sepals open up into large, very full, hybrid tea-shaped flowers of soft buttercream yellow with a tawny glow in their inner depths. Fully open flowers usually have a large button eye while the outer petals fade to nearly white and curl back into pointed tips. This results in a star-shaped flower—hence the French name, "Star of Lyon."

But it's the foliage that will really win you over. One gardener described it as simply the best greenery of any rose in her entire garden. I couldn't agree more. The leaves are composed of five to seven perfectly fashioned leaflets done up in rich olive green with a silvery reverse. They possess a quilted, puckered texture and have a wonderfully meaty substance about them. Blackspot is never an issue with this rose.

Owing to the impeccable foliage, this rose is especially useful in settings where a good-looking flowering shrub is needed. I'd love to see a row of 'Etoile de Lyon' lining the windows of a French café in Lake Worth or Coral Gables someday.

Hybridizer: Jean-Baptiste André Guillot
Culture: Easy
Availability: Moderate
Fragrance: Light
Average Size: 4–5' tall × 5–6' wide
Disease Resistance: Excellent
Rebloom: Excellent
Garden Uses: Flowerbeds, cut flowers, groupings, specimen, own-root

FAITH WHITTLESEY

Tea (Hybrid Gigantea), 2005

'Faith Whittlesey' is a little-known gem of a rose. I actually prefer the original name, 'Annapurna', which reflects the flowers' resemblance to the snowy massif in the Himalayas. The current name was chosen to honor the former U.S. ambassador to Switzerland, who herself was a zealous rose lover.

For a tea rose, this variety forms a compact shrub that stays around 4' tall and wide, perfect for smaller gardens. The wonderfully healthy foliage is spring green with gracefully pointed and drooping leaflet tips. Forked clusters of tapered buds open up into nodding, deeply cupped, pure white blossoms, occasionally graced with a yellowish to pinkish glow in their centers.

This rose is one of the rare few whose odor is actually unpleasant to me. I've sniffed 'Faith Whittlesey' many times, in many different contexts, and it smells like old, rancid dish soap every single time. The perception of fragrance is, of course, highly subjective, but several other gardeners have agreed with me on Faith's peculiar odor.

Don't let the scent scare you away, however. 'Faith Whittlesey' is one of the healthiest, heaviest-blooming roses I've ever seen in South Florida. A single specimen covered in flowers is a stunning sight in the garden—and in groupings, the color effect perfectly evokes the snowy mountain range that the original name honors.

Hybridizer: M. S. Viraraghavan
Culture: Easy
Availability: Wide
Fragrance: Unpleasant soapy smell
Average Size: 4' tall × 4' wide
Disease Resistance: Excellent
Rebloom: Excellent
Garden Uses: Flowerbeds, groupings, own-root, containers

FLO NELSON

Hybrid Tea, 2001

I am not a fan of orange flowers; luckily, 'Flo Nelson' is on the peachy side of orange. The petals are the color of the softest summer cantaloupe imaginable—mild and gentle, with just enough pastel yellow and pink mixed in to play well with many other garden colors. Try this one with rich blue salvias, sizzling scarlet ixoras, pale pink bougainvilleas, or deep black-purple cordylines. With 'Flo Nelson', the combinations are endless.

Flowers start out as long, shapely buds encapsulated with feathery sepals. These open up into high-centered, moderately full flowers with jaunty, wavy-edged petals that give off a delicious, warm, fruity tea fragrance. The fruity scent perfectly matches the peachy petal color. Disease resistance is good, and the rebloom on established plants is incredible.

This rose was named for the wife of Earl Nelson, a Hall of Fame recipient from the Florida Nursery Growers and Landscape Association. The FNGLA is North America's largest state-run nursery and landscape association; their annual Hall of Fame award is given out to an individual who demonstrated a lifetime of outstanding contributions to the landscape industry. Earl Nelson was all this and more: he devoted his entire professional life toward not just growing roses, but tirelessly promoting them as garden plants worthy of use throughout Florida.

Hybridizer: Mark Nelson
Culture: Easy
Availability: Moderate
Fragrance: Strong fruity/tea blend
Average Size: 5' tall × 4' wide
Disease Resistance: Good
Rebloom: Excellent
Garden Uses: Flowerbeds, cut flowers, groupings

FRANCIS DUBREUIL

Tea, 1894

No garden? No problem! 'Francis Dubreuil' is a pint-sized prince well suited to container gardening, so you can enjoy this rose even if you only have a sunny balcony or patio to work with.

Pointed purple-black buds open up into small, full, ruffled blooms of smoldering ruby with black smudging on the guard petals. They emit the powerful damask perfume you would expect from roses of this color. Petals can sometimes burn in the heat of midsummer, but they are usually fine the rest of the year.

'Francis Dubreuil' is one of the smallest tea roses available—mine has never exceeded 3' high. New canes are a gorgeous steel blue that contrasts nicely against the flowers. The glossy blue-green foliage is not as disease resistant as other teas, however, so this variety may need intervention to stay leafy.

There's currently a lot of confusion in the industry about whether what is being grown and sold as 'Francis Dubreuil' is actually another tea rose called 'Barcelona', which is virtually identical in size, habit, color, and fragrance. Kim Rupert, a volunteer at the Huntington Rose Garden in California, mentioned that the two varieties had to be planted in separate areas of their garden because of how consistently they confused both visitors and staff alike.

Many nurseries cannot guarantee a 100 percent positive ID on 'Francis Dubreuil', so bear that in mind when making your purchase.

Hybridizer: Francis Dubreuil
Culture: Somewhat challenging
Availability: Wide
Fragrance: Deep, rich damask
Average Size: 3' tall × 2–3' wide
Disease Resistance: Fair
Rebloom: Good
Garden Uses: Flowerbeds, cut flowers, groupings, containers, own-root

FRANCIS MEILLAND

Hybrid Tea, 1996

As a shrub, 'Francis Meilland' is difficult to use in the landscape—the canes are very thorny and shoot out at stiff, odd angles from the plant's base. However, the heart-melting flowers will make you quickly forget all that. Any bride who sees this rose will instantly want it for her wedding bouquet.

'Francis Meilland' beautifully exemplifies hybrid tea perfection: large buds, like finely cut jewels, subtended by leafy sepals that slowly unfurl into big, high-centered florists' roses of exquisite flawlessness. Each bloom, proudly displayed atop a cutting-length stem, is blessed with an intoxicating fruity aroma.

The color is somewhat of an enigma: too pink to really be white, but way too white to be listed as even a light pink rose. The delicate blush in each flower's center makes for an interesting juxtaposition against the thick, beefy petal substance and stalwart growth of the shrub itself. The overall effect is less damsel-in-distress and more tough-beauty—Wonder Woman reincarnated as a rose. The large, glossy leaves have very strong disease resistance.

The name commemorates Francis Meilland (1912–1958) one of the founding fathers of modern roses. Working for his family's namesake company in France, Francis bred the seedling of 'Peace', the most famous rose in history, which was released in 1945 upon the conclusion of World War II. Francis worked tirelessly to expand the Meilland business beyond France, bringing amazing new roses to gardeners worldwide.

Hybridizer: Alain Meilland
Culture: Easy
Availability: Wide
Fragrance: Outstanding, fruity
Average Size: 6' tall × 4' wide
Disease Resistance: Excellent
Rebloom: Excellent
Garden Uses: Flowerbeds, cut flowers, groupings

G. NABONNAND

Tea, 1888

The soft apricot-pink wash on 'G. Nabonnand's flowers is very similar to that of 'Princess Charlene de Monaco', but on a smaller, less symmetrical flower. The half-open flowers are handsome, shapely affairs, but mature blooms are a fray of lopsided, angular, flattened petals, like something out of a Picasso painting. They "finish up messy," as many gardeners put it.

Fortunately, 'G. Nabonnand' has a cornucopia of redeeming traits that overshadow this scruffy finish. Where do we start? Along with flawless disease resistance, this cultivar boasts 100 percent thornless stems and beautiful deep burgundy new growth. The shrub itself is rather airy textured, wonderful for use in mixed plantings. Last, a sweet-tea perfume emanates from the everblooming flowers. 'G. Nabonnand' has proven to be as wonderful in South Florida as 'Duchesse de Brabant'—both are problem-free, easy-to-grow roses, even for beginner gardeners.

If you can look past the flowers in their final moments, I guarantee 'G. Nabonnand' will become a garden favorite for you. Take advantage of this variety's open-textured, thornless growth by incorporating several in a mixed bed with 'Zinderella' zinnias, 'Kilimanjaro White' marigolds, and 'Mystic Spires' salvia. A border of African blue basil will complete the scene—and also offer plenty of sweet nectar for hungry bees passing by.

Hybridizer: Gilbert Nabonnand
Culture: Easy
Availability: Wide
Fragrance: Strong, sweet
Average Size: 5–6' tall × 5–6' wide
Disease Resistance: Excellent
Bloom Frequency: Excellent
Garden Uses: Flowerbeds, cut flowers, groupings, own-root

GOLD MEDAL

Grandiflora, 1982

Along with 'Love', 'Gold Medal' is a good beginner's rose simply because of the wide availability on 'Fortuniana' rootstock. For more experienced gardeners, however, there are better yellow roses worth taking the time and trouble to source. Gardeners should always deliberate if it's worth devoting your precious, limited garden space to an underwhelming plant.

A typical grandiflora, 'Gold Medal' forms a gangly, thorny, thick-caned shrub easily reaching 8' or taller without pruning. Leaves are a textured medium green and have poor disease resistance in my observations. Admittedly, the just-opened flowers are lovely—big, shapely blooms of golden yellow gently kissed with pink and bronze. Unfortunately, as the flowers age, they pale to a sickly buff-ivory hue, and the pink tones spread significantly.

Every so often, I'll be asked to identify a light yellow rose growing on an old, mostly defoliated shrub—and every time, it turns out to be 'Gold Medal'. The wan, almost jaundiced tone of these blooms in their final moments is an easy marker for this variety, and, oddly enough, it's only ever this stage of the flower's development that is shown to me for identification.

Certainly, 'Gold Medal' is a rose well suited to *survive* in South Florida, but I've never seen one really *thriving* here. This is one of several garden plants—not just roses—whose owner frequently describes it as "an old favorite," but I can't help thinking, "Why?"

Hybridizer: Jack E. Christensen
Culture: Easy
Availability: Wide
Fragrance: Medium, rosy
Average Size: 7–8' tall × 5' wide
Disease Resistance: Fair
Rebloom: Good
Garden Uses: Flowerbeds, cut flowers, groupings

GRANADA

Hybrid Tea, 1963

One of the traits endemic to China roses (and their hybrid tea descendants) is their "suntanning" ability: petal colors can darken, or even change completely, with exposure to sunlight. 'Granada' suntans like she's spending the summer on South Beach. These color-changing blooms burn like hot coals in the garden, and their perfume is truly orgasmic.

Long, sculpted buds with handsome sepals spiral open into high-centered, semidouble blooms endowed with a powerful old-rose-and-spice perfume. The petals, at first glance, appear as a fiery shade of red commonly called "nasturtium." If you look closely, however, you'll see that the red tones are confined to the outer edges of the flower while their centers are a blend of tangerine and hot pink. The red tones will then spread out and darken over time—the aforementioned "suntanning."

Flowers produced in the heat of summer are just as colorful as winter blooms but tend to be smaller and open quickly. The foliage is distinctive: dark green, semipendant, and wavy textured, strongly reminiscent of holly leaves.

'Granada' stays relatively compact at around 5' tall, one of the smaller hybrid teas for South Florida. One negative I've noticed over the years is that this rose tends to grow random inward canes, which can lead to congestion-induced blackspot. Remove these canes as you spot them to promote a more open-centered shrub with better airflow.

Hybridizer: Robert V. Lindquist
Culture: Easy
Availability: Wide
Fragrance: Outstanding, spicy old rose
Average Size: 5' tall × 4' wide
Disease Resistance: Good
Rebloom: Good
Garden Uses: Flowerbeds, cut flowers, groupings

GRANDE DAME

Hybrid Tea, 2011

In all of my gardens, I always include at least one damask-scented rose for cut flowers. My first choice in Oakland Park was 'Neil Diamond', but—for me, anyway—it was a blackspot magnet that rarely flowered. Roses that are both unhealthy and stingy bloomers are hard to justify taking up valuable garden space and usually end up shovel pruned. Such was Neil's fate.

But the show must go on! After 'Neil Diamond' left the stage, I immediately searched for a replacement act. I settled on 'Grande Dame' after just one whiff at a nursery. This rose does get some blackspot, but not nearly as badly as its predecessor. Moreover, 'Grande Dame' is a much more vigorous grower than 'Neil Diamond', rapidly forming a tall, upright, thorny shrub that replaces diseased leaves quickly. The dark green leaflets are attractively wavy and have drooping tips, lending a sense of gracefulness to the bulky plant.

'Grande Dame' is part grandiflora in lineage and produces flowers in typically grandiflora-ish sprays of three to five. Long reddish buds with elegant sepals open up into really large (5–6"), broadly cupped flowers of rich fuchsia. The outer petals reflex over 180 degrees as the flower matures, resulting in an enormous, peony-like bloom that simply commands attention. Combined with the intense damask perfume and long cutting stems, this variety is a must-have for those who primarily grow roses for cutting.

Hybridizer: Tom Carruth
Culture: Easy
Availability: Wide
Fragrance: Rich damask
Average Size: 6–7' tall × 4–5' wide
Disease Resistance: Good
Rebloom: Good
Garden Uses: Flowerbeds, cut flowers, groupings

HAYWOOD HALL

Noisette, 2007

'Haywood Hall' is the most intensely fragrant of all the "true" Noisettes that I've trialed—I say "true" Noisettes to distinguish them from the larger-flowered tea-Noisettes. These blossoms, typically in giant domed clusters of 30 or more, are richly perfumed with a robust distillation that smells exactly like a warm cup of tea mixed with sugar, lemon, and cream—strong and sweet, but refreshing rather than overpowering.

Flowers, emerging from pointed pink buds, are pale blush fading to white. Petals are slender and oval to strap shaped, like many of the "true" Noisettes. Rebloom is fabulous virtually all year long on established plants.

The shrub itself is also typical of the original Noisettes: an arching to sprawling mass of flexible canes that make it a good choice for an arch or obelisk. Leaves are composed of slender, pastel green leaflets with good disease resistance. 'Haywood Hall' responds extremely well to topdressings of rotted manure, especially when a bloom flush is eminent.

This fragrant delight was named for the historic home in Raleigh, North Carolina, where it was first discovered in 2007. The two-story Federal-style mansion served as the home of John Haywood, who became the first state treasurer of North Carolina in 1787—a position he held for the next 40 years until his death in 1827. He remains the state's longest-serving treasurer to date.

Discoverer: Charles Walker
Culture: Easy
Availability: Moderate
Fragrance: Strong, spicy tea
Average Size: 7–15' tall × 5–10' wide
Disease Resistance: Good
Bloom Frequency: Excellent
Garden Uses: Medium climber, cut flowers, groupings, specimen, light
  shade, own-root, pollinators

HELGA'S QUEST

Shrub (Hybrid Gigantea), 2015

'Helga's Quest' is one of several excellent releases from Indian breeder M. S. Viraraghavan. Viraraghavan's goal was to develop roses fully suited to the humid tropical climate of his native India; 100-odd cultivars later, he has most definitely succeeded in that mission. It's only natural that we here in equally humid South Florida would want to explore his creations.

Although classed as a shrub rose, 'Helga's Quest' more strongly resembles a hybrid tea with stiff, upright growth and long cutting-length stems. The plant exhibits dense, symmetrical branching from the ground up, making it useful as a small specimen plant. The healthy foliage is glossy bright green with a bronzy tint—a nice backdrop for the vivid flowers.

The cup-shaped blooms are jubilant, multicolored concoctions. No two flowers are exactly alike, and their tones vary widely, but the general theme is creamy yellow liberally flushed with deep coral pink and a warm apricot inner glow. At times, the yellow tones increase so much that the blooms could be mistaken for another variety entirely. Strong sunlight can cause the guard petals to develop bright red feathering along their tips.

'Helga's Quest' is somewhat hard to come by, especially on 'Fortuniana' rootstock—which you'd definitely want, as this variety is not naturally nematode resistant. This is another rose that reminds us of what it means to be a gardener—that is to say, patient with a capital P.

Hybridizer: M. S. Viraraghavan
Culture: Easy
Availability: Limited
Fragrance: Light
Average Size: 5–6' tall × 4' wide
Disease Resistance: Good
Rebloom: Excellent
Garden Uses: Flowerbeds, cut flowers, groupings, specimen

HERITAGE (JOSEPHINE LAND)

Shrub (David Austin), 1982

Beautiful, fragrant, and usually available, 'Heritage' is an English rose that performs wonderfully in South Florida, especially in partial shade. I situated five plants on the east side of our Oakland Park house, where they were fully shaded from about 2:00 p.m. onward: their show was always spectacular.

Also called 'Josephine Land', 'Heritage' forms an arching, spreading shrub best used as either a small climber or in groupings of three, so that the tangle of canes will interlock to form one large mass. The undulate leaflets are a beautiful dark green with a semiglossy sheen. Canes are almost 100 percent thornless—a great rose for siting near walkways or other high-traffic areas.

Flowers are produced in long-stemmed sprays of conical buds. These open up into light pink, perfectly round blooms shaped like camellias with concentric layers of petals. Blooms are blessed with a strong, lemony old-rose aroma. Bees seem to find these flowers irresistible. I've frequently also found zebra longwings and Gulf fritillaries perching on the open flowers—I say "perching" because it's hard to tell if the butterflies are actually drinking or just relaxing.

'Heritage' has only one real flaw: the flowers shatter quickly, usually by their third day, which limits their usefulness for arrangements. To me, however, their short-lived nature just makes these beauties all the more precious. I love cutting half-opened sprigs of 'Heritage', arranging them in a casual bouquet with 'Coral Nymph' salvia and blue mistflower, and enjoying their brief romance together.

Hybridizer: David Austin
Culture: Easy
Availability: Wide
Fragrance: Strong old rose/lemon blend
Average Size: 5–8' tall × 4–6' wide
Disease Resistance: Good
Rebloom: Excellent
Garden Uses: Flowerbeds, cut flowers, groupings, small climber, partial shade, pollinators

ICEBERG

Floribunda, 1958

'Iceberg's creator probably had no idea that this simple shrub would go on to become the most widely planted white rose in history. Like some kind of floral Godfather, 'Iceberg' has also spawned a huge, far-reaching family. It has produced several beautiful mutations—'Climbing Iceberg', 'Pink Iceberg', 'Burgundy Iceberg'—that have all become popular varieties in their own right. 'Iceberg' has also been used in countless breeding programs over the years, most notably by David Austin. Dozens of the best English roses have 'Iceberg' as a parent, as do hundreds of other splendid roses worldwide.

This is largely due to 'Iceberg's impressive set of traits: strong growth, strong disease resistance, nonstop bloom, partial shade tolerance, and flowers that drop cleanly without deadheading. Individual blooms are modest, flattened cups with an unremarkable scent. But because they always come in clusters, mature plants give an excellent color effect. Each blossom is anchored with lemon-yellow stamens that age to dark gray—a somber but elegant color pairing not seen in many other roses. The graceful, upright-ascending canes form a handsome shrub cloaked in glossy green foliage.

I used six 'Iceberg's in a curved planting along our large bay kitchen window in our Cape Coral garden. On cool winter mornings, with coffee in hand, the windows open, and a gentle breeze rustling both the curtains and the roses beyond them, I momentarily get the sense that all is right in the world.

Hybridizer: Reimer Kordes
Culture: Easy
Availability: Wide
Fragrance: Medium, sweet
Average Size: 5–8' tall × 5–8' wide
Disease Resistance: Good
Rebloom: Excellent
Garden Uses: Flowerbeds, cut flowers, groupings, hedge, pollinators,
    partial shade

JUDE THE OBSCURE

Shrub (David Austin), 1995

From the first time I encountered 'Jude the Obscure', I knew that this was a rose I could never afterward live without. The fact that it's well suited to South Florida's humid heat just seals the deal. David Austin released countless apricot-colored roses over his long career, but 'Jude the Obscure' is the best in my opinion.

Large rounded buds, typically in sprays, slowly expand into warm apricot-yellow blooms with a grapefruit-pink glow. They are so deeply incurved that they appear more like tulips than roses; the flowers hold this convex shape right up until shattering. Their soft coloration mingles well with countless other colors in the garden. New growth is a tender reddish brown, maturing to rich blue-green, oval leaflets that nicely blanket the spreading canes.

But it's the fragrance that is really the pièce de résistance here: 'Jude the Obscure' is one of the most deliciously perfumed roses ever created. The blooms smell exactly like freshly cut grapefruit—sharp, sweet, and intensely citrusy, without the spicy jasmine-like finish typical of other citrus-scented roses. Words don't do it proper justice; you simply have to smell for yourself to understand. But do so with the knowledge that one sniff may result in a lifetime love affair.

This rose is named after the tragic main character in Thomas Hardy's novel of the same name. Hardy, a Victorian-era novelist and poet, frequently wrote about the social constraints of the Victorian era and how they adversely affected the people of his time.

Hybridizer: David Austin
Culture: Easy
Availability: Moderate
Fragrance: Powerful, pervasive grapefruit
Average Size: 5–6' tall × 4–5' wide
Disease Resistance: Good
Rebloom: Excellent
Garden Uses: Flowerbeds, cut flowers, groupings

JULIA CHILD

Floribunda, 2004

Named for the famous chef who popularized French cuisine in America, 'Julia Child' is a dependably small rose in South Florida—the rounded shrub never exceeds 4' in height or spread. Thorny stems covered in glossy green leaves create the perfect backdrop for the endless parade of full, stiffly ruffled, 3" golden-yellow flowers. Pointed buds, typically in short-stemmed clusters of three, are produced nonstop all year long here.

The flowers have a distinctive licorice fragrance that is strongest during midmorning. As the blooms age, they fade to pale lemon yellow before dropping. Bees simply adore the flowers, so this is definitely one to include in a pollinator garden.

I love 'Julia Child' more for its versatility than anything else—this rose can be used in almost any landscape situation you can think of. Flowerbeds, mass plantings, containers, or even as an everblooming low hedge—the possibilities are many. The short stems are too small for most vases, but if you get creative with your containers (an elegant coffee creamer, for example), 'Julia Child' makes excellent cut flowers with a long vase life and delectable scent.

Julia Carolyn Child (née McWilliams, 1912) died in 2004 at the age of 91 after a lifetime of achievements and accolades, including the U.S. Presidential Medal of Freedom and the French Legion of Honour. Her last book, *My Life in France,* ends with her reflection: "Thinking back on it now reminds me that the pleasures of the table, and of life, are infinite—*toujours bon appétit!*"

Hybridizer: Tom Carruth
Culture: Easy
Availability: Wide
Fragrance: Strong licorice
Average Size: 3–4' tall × 3–4' wide
Disease Resistance: Good
Rebloom: Excellent
Garden Uses: Flowerbeds, cut flowers, groupings, hedge, containers, pollinators

KEY WEST ROCK ROSE

Tea, unknown

The now-shuttered Giles Rose Nursery of Central Florida once acquired a tea rose that they thought was 'Mrs. Dudley Cross' but soon realized their mistake: 'Mrs. Dudley Cross' is a thornless rose while what they had on their hands definitely had more than a few prickles. Nursery owner Jim Giles traced it back to a friend in Key West who gave them the original specimen and then decided to release it into commerce as the 'Key West Rock Rose.'

"Rocky," as I affectionately call this one, produces slender, twiggy canes that eventually form a dense shrub around 4' tall but much wider in spread, with a distinctly horizontal branching habit. The tender, sepia-colored new growth ages to semiglossy dark green. Leaves are usually composed of just three rhomboid-shaped leaflets and have excellent disease resistance.

Tapered buds, either single stemmed or in small sprays, open up into 2", unscented, creamy white blossoms shaded with apricot orange in their centers and deep pink on the tips. The crimped petals don't really have any organization to them but instead appear to spread out in random directions, creating a delightfully informal, fluffy-looking flower.

The flowers' small size is exacerbated by the fact that this variety is never covered in bloom at any one time, unlike most other tea roses. But I keep Rocky around simply because of its obscure origins and iron-clad constitution. Few roses are better able to withstand oppressive heat, humidity, poor soil, and general neglect—and for that reason I'd always give this underdog a safe place to call home.

Discoverer: Jim and Diann Giles
Culture: Easy
Availability: Moderate
Fragrance: None
Average Size: 4–5' tall × 5–6' wide
Disease Resistance: Excellent
Rebloom: Fair
Garden Uses: Flowerbeds, cut flowers, groupings, hedge, own-root, conversation piece

LA MARNE

Polyantha, 1915

During my first ten years in South Florida, I constantly saw a bright pink, cluster-flowering rose simply labeled as "Pink Rose" in several Miami-area nurseries. I never actually bought any for myself—mainly because I tend to shy away from purchasing unnamed varieties. I'm more than a little regretful that it took ten years for me to finally experience this awesome little rose for myself. But as Henry David Thoreau said, "To regret deeply is to live afresh."

A typical polyantha, 'La Marne' is a bushy, spreading plant with glossy green foliage exhibiting good disease resistance. Big, multibranched clusters of buds turn into small, cup-shaped blooms with two or three rows of wavy-edged petals. They are pale pink edged in deep rose with prominent gold-brown stamens.

Although the bicolor effect is elegant when viewed up close, from a distance the flowers appear a uniform bright pink. Combined with the huge flowering trusses, a mature plant in full bloom is a wonderful drench of pink in the landscape. The blooms are usually swarming with hungry bees on a mission, so definitely include 'La Marne' if you're planning a pollinator garden.

Overall, this is a charming, easy-to-grow South Florida rose, especially useful for commercial settings, large beds, and any other situations where a big splash of low-maintenance color is desired.

Hybridizer: Barbier Frères & Compagnie
Culture: Easy
Availability: Wide
Fragrance: Light
Average Size: 4' tall × 4–6' wide
Disease Resistance: Excellent
Rebloom: Excellent
Garden Uses: Flowerbeds, cut flowers, groupings, hedge, pollinators,
 Earth-Kind®, own-root

LADY OF MEGGINCH

Shrub (David Austin), 2007

I categorized 'Lady of Megginch' as "somewhat challenging" not because this variety is especially weak or disease prone but because, habitwise, the shrub is neither here nor there. The sinuous canes are too floppy to make a self-supporting shrub, yet they don't really want to climb either. The best approach is to plant 'Lady of Megginch' in small groupings so that the canes interweave to create a more stable mound of greenery.

Very round, plump buds the color of cherry tomatoes have elegant foliated sepals. These explode into big, rounded, flattened rosettes of a saturated warm pink that lightens in the hot summer months. Flowers are crammed with petals in a gorgeous old-rose formation and give off a delicious papaya fragrance.

New growth is a tender spring green that matures to slate green with a bluish tinge. There is a delicate translucency to the rounded leaflets—this is a rose that should ideally be positioned so that late afternoon sunlight can shine through it.

Born in 1928, Cherry Drummond, the 16th Baroness Strange, lived in the Scottish castle of Megginch until her death in 2005. This rose commemorates her efforts as president of the War Widows Association of Great Britain, a resource and advocacy group for the surviving spouses of military personnel killed in battle.

Hybridizer: David Austin
Culture: Somewhat challenging
Availability: Moderate
Fragrance: Strong, fruity aroma
Average Size: 5–6' tall × 4–6' wide
Disease Resistance: Good
Rebloom: Excellent
Garden Uses: Flowerbeds, cut flowers, groupings, small climber

LE VÉSUVE

China, 1825

Though classed as a China rose, 'Le Vésuve' is decidedly un-China-like in appearance: the foliage is thicker than the average China, and the high-centered flowers look more like tea roses. Many rosarians argue that this variety should be reclassed as a tea rose, but for now it remains a China.

'Le Vésuve' forms a dense, upright-rounded, vigorous-growing shrub. New growth is light reddish mahogany, maturing to semiglossy dark green; the drooping leaflets are broadly oval with tapered tips. Flower buds are deep fuchsia pink, opening up into big (for a China), florist-style, carnation-pink roses with lilac tones, similar to 'Belinda's Dream' but with looser, more translucent petals.

Although 'Le Vésuve's buds are initially upright, mature flowers usually dangle from their weight. Some people dislike this "nodding" aspect of old roses, but I adore it. The accompanying tea fragrance is sweet, cool, and refreshing.

Like many Chinas and teas, 'Le Vésuve' is armed with big, curved, painfully sharp thorns. In the wild, these help the plant climb over nearby competitors; in the landscaping world, they work well to discourage pedestrian traffic. If you have unwanted people coming into your yard, plant a hedge of 'Le Vésuve' and see if that doesn't solve the problem—in the most picturesque manner, of course.

Hybridizer: Jean Laffay
Culture: Easy
Availability: Wide
Fragrance: Medium tea
Average Size: 4–5' tall × 4–6' wide
Disease Resistance: Good
Rebloom: Good
Garden Uses: Flowerbeds, cut flowers, groupings, hedge, own-root

LEMON SPICE

Hybrid Tea, 1966

There is perhaps no more fitting name for a rose than 'Lemon Spice', as it perfectly describes both the pastel color and the tantalizing citrus aroma. Since my first whiff of 'Lemon Spice' years ago, I've always felt that this rose smells exactly like lemon bars fresh out of the oven—warm and tart and oh so sweet.

The half-opened buds on 'Lemon Spice' are so long and chiseled that they remind me of seahorses or hummingbirds. Cool weather brings out soft peach shading, but for the rest of the year the blooms are light yellow fading to white. Mature flowers are fluffy and antique in appearance, often so heavy that they droop downward. A relatively small hybrid tea in South Florida, its prickly canes are lined with matte dark green leaves.

'Lemon Spice' is not for low-maintenance gardens—blackspot can be a problem—but the fragrance alone makes me include at least one in any garden that I own. Position this one in a spot you'll walk past daily, such as the front door or back patio. My favorite companion flower is just a simple planting of 'Gold Mound' lantana: the dark yellow lantana blossoms perfectly highlight the pale yellow of 'Lemon Spice', and the lantana's citrus-scented foliage underscores the rose's citrus-scented flowers.

Hybridizer: David L. Armstrong
Culture: Somewhat challenging
Availability: Moderate
Fragrance: Powerful sweet citrus
Average Size: 4–5' tall × 4–5' wide
Disease Resistance: Fair
Rebloom: Excellent
Garden Uses: Flowerbeds, cut flowers, groupings

LOUIS-PHILIPPE

China, 1834

No book on South Florida roses would be complete without 'Louis-Philippe'. He's so popular here that he's often simply called "the Florida rose" by gardeners and professionals alike. This crimson crusader comes in strong with nonstop rebloom, flawless health, and wide availability—all on a vigorous, zero-maintenance plant. If any rose could be said to thrive on neglect, this is it.

Although frequently confused with 'Agrippina', 'Louis-Philippe' can be distinguished by his rounder flowers that have noticeably pinkish centers. 'Louis-Philippe' also has a much stronger fragrance, evocative of bell peppers and tea. Both varieties produce their bright flowers in much the same way: forked sprays of upright to nodding buds.

'Louis-Philippe' is a hefty shrub, easily attaining a 10' height and spread without pruning to keep it smaller. The dark green, pointed leaves are 100 percent disease-proof, while the sharp, hooked thorns make for an excellent barrier hedge. Cuttings root easily, rendering this rose a good choice for gardeners on a budget.

This rose commemorates Louis Philippe I, the last king of France, who ruled from 1830 to 1848. Emily de Zavala, the wife of the Mexican minister to France at the time, fell in love with this variety while visiting the king's court in the 1830s, and she brought samples back to North America. It quickly became so widely grown across Mexico that it was temporarily known as the Zavala rose.

Hybridizer: Modeste Guérin
Culture: Easy
Availability: Wide
Fragrance: Sharp, peppery
Average Size: 5–10' tall × 5–10' wide
Disease Resistance: Excellent
Rebloom: Excellent
Garden Uses: Flowerbeds, cut flowers, groupings, hedge, specimen, own-root

LOVE

Grandiflora, 1980

I do not "love" this rose. The mature flowers are not the epitome of floral beauty; and lack of fragrance is never a great thing in my book. But 'Love' is readily available on 'Fortuniana' rootstock in countless garden centers throughout South Florida, which makes for a great beginner's rose—no need to seek out a fancy nursery or wait for an online shipment to arrive.

Unlike most grandifloras, 'Love' produces flowers one per stem typically. The partially opened buds are gorgeous: tight cones of frosty white with reddish-fuchsia tips that scroll back to create a peppermint effect. Unfortunately, mature flowers are flat, shapeless bundles of dull red petals, and the candy-striped effect is completely lost. Especially from a distance, they simply appear as nondescript red roses at this point. Mature plants do have good rebloom though.

'Love' is a good South Florida rose simply because it grows so well in our climate. But be sure to select companion plants carefully—'Love's matte green foliage and dull red flowers are easily overwhelmed by flashier landscape fare. Try using 'Love' in front of a silver buttonwood hedge, underplanted with a mix of magenta, pink, and white pentas. This will create a delicate, Candyland-esque color story that 'Love's red and (fleeting) white tones will look right at home in.

Hybridizer: William Warriner
Culture: Easy
Availability: Wide
Fragrance: None
Average Size: 5–6' tall × 4' wide
Disease Resistance: Fair
Rebloom: Good
Garden Uses: Flowerbeds, cut flowers, groupings

LOVE SONG

Floribunda, 2011

Along with 'Poseidon', 'Love Song' is one of the newer lavender releases that has really gone a long way toward redeeming this color group as a whole. The older mauve and lavender roses were notoriously weak growers riddled with disease, even when given the best of care. Not so with 'Love Song'—this one's at the top of my list for gardeners seeking a good lavender.

Really big (4–5") blooms of truly exquisite hybrid-tea form swirl open from clusters of pointed, raspberry-purple buds with chartreuse shading. Their color is a rich, dreamy lilac shaded darker toward each flower's center. Much like 'Poseidon', the flowers are handsome from start to finish, assuming a cabbage-like old-rose look right before shattering. The fragrance is moderate at best, but it's a small tradeoff for the sumptuous blooms. The shrub itself is thorny, rounded upright in outline, and well clothed in dark green leaves. New growth is brilliant ruby red, giving the shrub extra color appeal periodically.

'Love Song' is not as disease resistant as 'Poseidon'—I can't think of many other lavenders that are—but is still light-years beyond older members of this color group in terms of health. For a particularly potent purple palette, place a grouping of 'Love Song' in a bed with pale purple agastache, dark blue torenia, and a violet-flowered tropical lilac (*Cornutia grandiflora*) as a background anchor.

Hybridizer: Tom Carruth
Culture: Easy
Availability: Wide
Fragrance: Light, sweet
Average Size: 4–5' tall × 4–5' wide
Disease Resistance: Good
Rebloom: Excellent
Garden Uses: Flowerbeds, cut flowers, groupings

LYDA ROSE

Shrub (Hybrid Musk), 1994

'Lyda Rose' was the first five-petaled rose that I ever grew in South Florida and the one that sparked my love affair with single roses in general. Like all other single roses, the blossoms are very attractive to pollinators—a wonderful thing in today's eco-minded gardening world.

The flower effect of a mature 'Lyda Rose' in full bloom is exactly like a northern apple tree in its springtime splendor—a diaphanous cloud of tenderest pink and white. Flowers come in large, airy clusters of anywhere from 10 to 50 small, pointed, dark pink buds. These open up to 1", blush-colored flowers with lilac pink on the reverse of each petal and a central mass of golden stamens.

The canes are bristly with hundreds of small prickles that look deceptively soft (they aren't—be warned). Long, slender leaflets are medium green with a silvery reverse. As with most of the hybrid musks, 'Lyda Rose' tolerates partial shade and will succeed in semishady spots that would spell doom for other roses.

'Lyda Rose' forms a dense, sprawling shrub with a fountain-like habit of growth that lends itself to countless landscape uses. Wild-rose-esque varieties like this one also have a special magic because they appear both humble and elegant at the same time—not an easy task for any flower to pull off. Try placing a pair of 'Lyda Rose' in matching obelisks framing the entrance to a garden area. The play of color, texture, and opacity will imprint in your mind forever.

Hybridizer: Kleine Lettunich
Culture: Easy
Availability: Moderate
Fragrance: Light, sweet
Average Size: 6–9' tall × 6–9' wide
Disease Resistance: Good
Rebloom: Excellent
Garden Uses: Flowerbeds, cut flowers, groupings, hedge, small climber, own-root, partial shade, pollinators

MADAME ALFRED CARRIÈRE

Tea-Noisette, 1875

When my original 2-gallon specimen of 'Madame Alfred Carrière' first arrived, it was left in its pot for over six weeks while I vacillated on where to plant her. By the time I selected just the right spot, the canes—which had been pruned down to maybe 10" for shipping—had shot out to over 3' tall and had flower buds forming. Many gorgeous roses are agonizingly slow growing, so it's refreshing to come upon those that give instant gratification *and* long-term beauty.

Long, pale pink buds with reddish sepals expand into 3–4", ivory-white, teacup-shaped blooms with a warm glow in their inner depths. Although technically a semidouble rose, the inner petals are so folded and crimped that the illusion of a fully double flower is created. The fragrance, a sweet blend of old rose and tea, is especially strong in winter. Foliage is light spring green with good blackspot resistance.

'MAC', as this rose is commonly abbreviated, will grow to 20' or more in length and spread, so give this one ample room from the get-go; it deeply resents pruning. 'MAC's yellowish canes are almost 100 percent thornless, making this rose especially user-friendly for training. Owing to its thornlessness, 'MAC' is also a perfect climber for use near pedestrian areas: draped over a front porch, spanning a garage trellis, or covering a back yard pergola.

Hybridizer: Joseph Schwartz
Culture: Easy
Availability: Wide
Fragrance: Strong old rose/tea blend
Average Size: 20–25' tall × 10–20' wide
Disease Resistance: Good
Rebloom: Excellent
Garden Uses: Large climber, cut flowers, light shade, own-root

MADAME DRIOUT

Tea, 1903

Along with 'Moser Pink Striped', 'Madame Driout' is one of the few striped tea roses in commerce—but unlike 'Moser', this variety forms a pretty large plant. If you have space to accommodate a hefty climber, your reward will be some amazing colors coupled with a tantalizing perfume.

'Madame Driout' is a flamboyant showoff of a rose: large cylindrical buds that explode into enormous, loose, cupped flowers of cool pink randomly striped and splotched with raspberry red. The petal reverses are almost completely red; in combination with their scrolled and curled edges, the painterly effect is a beautiful, sophisticated sight to behold. The blooms' sweet fragrance smells exactly like watermelon Jolly Ranchers® to me. Cool season flowers have a higher petal count than warm weather blooms and are sometimes attractively quartered.

Like many climbers, 'Madame Driout' may take several months to fully settle into the garden. When it finally does, expect this rose to throw out long, thick, red-tinted canes studded with hooked thorns. Flowers tend to come in branching clusters shooting off the main canes.

The Madame's large, medium green leaves have reddish petioles and a uniquely soft, papery texture. But disease resistance is not as strong as for some of the other tea roses in South Florida, so consider spraying if you want to keep 'Madame Driout' leafy at all times.

Hybridizer: J. Thiriat
Culture: Easy
Availability: Moderate
Fragrance: Strong, sweet candy
Average Size: 12–20' tall × 8–15' wide
Disease Resistance: Fair
Rebloom: Good
Garden Uses: Large climber, cut flowers, own-root

MADAME JOSEPH SCHWARTZ

Tea, 1880

A pale sport of 'Duchesse de Brabant', 'Madame Joseph Schwartz' is identical in every way except color. Both form dense, twiggy shrubs well clothed in disease-proof olive green foliage and sparse-but-sharp, downward-hooked thorns. They both also share the same delectable apricots-and-allspice perfume that is just as strong in the evening as it is at dawn.

Pointed, pale green and pink buds open up into 3" cups of tender blush-ivory with ethereal pink shading along the petal tips. Just like the parent plant, 'Madame Joseph Schwartz' typically blooms in loose, open sprays of three to seven flowers that are large and full in cool weather, smaller and less double with summer heat. They usually nod horizontally but occasionally face upward on vigorous new shoots.

This variety's petals are perhaps the most translucent of any rose I've ever grown. They are so thin and sheer that they light up like lanterns when backlit by anything: sunlight, lamps, candles, smartphones, you name it. Plant 'Madame Joseph Schwartz' in a spot where late afternoon sun will shine directly through the plant for an enchanting play of light and shadow that will leave you speechless.

Hybridizer: Joseph Schwartz
Culture: Easy
Availability: Wide
Fragrance: Strong allspice/apricot blend
Average Size: 5–6' tall × 5' wide
Disease Resistance: Excellent
Rebloom: Excellent
Garden Uses: Flowerbeds, cut flowers, groupings, hedge, specimen, own-root, pollinators

MAGGIE

Bourbon/China, 1910

No other rose has left as many scars on my forearms as 'Maggie'. The mixed Bourbon/China heritage of this rose is evident in its massive, hooked, viciously sharp thorns. Owing to the bloodthirsty prickles and large size of mature plants, 'Maggie' works wonders as a barrier hedge. Forget expensive security systems—just plant a few 'Maggie's around your home and watch the would-be trespassers limp away. Only a fool would try to walk through a hedge of this rose.

Flowers are usually in tight, nodding clusters of two to four on long stems. Oval buds open up into full, 3" rosettes packed with small, folded petals; the outer petals reflex to create a peony-like effect. The color is lost somewhere between deep pink and light red; we'll call it cerise to make life simple. 'Maggie's fragrance is a medium old-rose scent with a peppery overtone, and for some odd (but wonderful) reason, it gets noticeably stronger when flowers are cut and brought indoors. The dark green, downward-curled, almost sinister-looking leaves are 100 percent disease-proof for me.

This rose has many aliases: 'Madame Eugene Marlitt', 'Bao Xiang', 'Bermuda Pacific', 'Kakinada Red', and 'Zi Yan Fei Wu' are a few other names it's sold under. I've always just preferred 'Maggie', however—it's short, simple, and easy to spell. But no matter what name you choose, this rose is a must-have for any South Florida garden—especially if you want to keep people *out* of *your* South Florida garden.

Hybridizer: Unknown
Culture: Easy
Availability: Wide
Fragrance: Peppery old rose
Average Size: 7–10' tall × 7–10' wide
Disease Resistance: Excellent
Rebloom: Excellent
Garden Uses: Flowerbeds, cut flowers, groupings, hedge, own-root

MARCHESA BOCCELLA

Hybrid Perpetual, 1842

'Marchesa Boccella' is frequently described as one of the few hybrid perpetuals that lives up to the group name. This holds true in South Florida where we tend to get two massive flushes—one in March, another near Thanksgiving—plus scattered blooms the rest of the year.

Also known as 'Jacques Cartier', this beauty forms a broom-like mass of slender, bristly canes that usually flop over from the weight of the flowers. The foliage is unique among roses: lance-shaped to almost rhomboidal, dark green leaflets with a pearly sheen. Disease resistance is average in South Florida.

Flowers are usually produced in tight clusters of three to five plump, rounded buds with beautifully fringed sepals. These open into full, flattened rosettes of soft light pink with a button eye. Petals are slender and strap shaped, providing a wonderful textural contrast to the many broad-petaled roses in South Florida. The flowers' potent old-rose fragrance wafts deliciously in our humid air.

'Marchesa Boccella' seems to do well with morning sun and afternoon shade, although it can also tolerate full sun positions. And though this shrub can get hefty, I know of one West Palm Beach gardener who successfully grew hers in a large ceramic pot on her patio where the incredible fragrance could be most easily enjoyed.

Discoverer: Jean Desprez
Culture: Easy
Availability: Moderate
Fragrance: Strong old rose
Average Size: 5–6' tall × 4–6' wide
Disease Resistance: Fair
Bloom Frequency: Good
Garden Uses: Flowerbeds, cut flowers, groupings

MARINETTE

Shrub (David Austin), 1995

"Joyous" is the best word to describe 'Marinette'. I can't think of many other roses that replicate the cheerful effect created when 'Marinette' is covered with twirling buds and flowers, looking for all the world like a troupe of tiny cancan dancers. Another perk: this is one of the few Austins that grows well in South Florida as an own-root shrub.

Shapely pink buds, usually in large sprays, have layers of petals perfectly spiraled like a conch shell. These unfurl into very blousy, open-faced blooms with crimped and scalloped petals done up in a wash of soft pink and white. Reddish new growth matures to medium green, wavy-textured foliage with good disease resistance. 'Marinette' can get large, so plan for a shrub in the 6–8' range.

'Marinette's blooms strongly remind me of Brazilian clusia (*Clusia orthoneura*), a tropical shrub with similar open-faced flowers of porcelainlike delicacy—in fact, the other common name for Brazilian clusia is porcelain flower. I've grown *C. orthoneura* and, while the blooms are striking, they occur infrequently at best. A mature specimen of 'Marinette', on the other hand, can be completely covered in flowers during a flush. Like most single and semi-double roses, the blossoms are also attractive to pollinators, adding another layer of delight to this already wonderful variety.

Hybridizer: David Austin
Culture: Easy
Availability: Moderate
Fragrance: Light
Average Size: 6–7' tall × 5–7' wide
Disease Resistance: Good
Rebloom: Good
Garden Uses: Flowerbeds, cut flowers, groupings, own-root, pollinators

MARTHA'S VINEYARD

Shrub, 1995

I've grown increasingly fond of 'Martha's Vineyard' over the years, especially for landscape projects requiring low-maintenance beauty. For those seeking loads of brilliant color on a hassle-free plant, you don't need to look much further than this one.

'Martha's Vineyard' is one of the more handsome roses from a foliage perspective. Expect a low, wide-spreading mound of small, bright green, fernlike leaves with wonderful disease resistance. The pliable canes are covered in minute, bristly thorns that are deceptively soft looking but will inflict painful scratches if you handle them without gloves.

Individual blossoms are tiny—barely 1" across—and deep watermelon pink with a small white blotch. But because they come in big clusters of up to 40 buds, a mature plant is a lovely wash of vibrant pink. Like most single roses, the flowers are attractive to all sorts of pollinators.

This willowy rose is wonderful for filling up large areas with color and works great as a groundcover plant. Or try using a single specimen trained as a small climber: the flowering laterals will dangle like a cascading fountain of deep pink. A rotation of seasonal annuals planted underneath give ever-changing garden effects throughout the year.

Hybridizer: L. Pernille Olesen
Culture: Easy
Availability: Wide
Fragrance: None
Average Size: 3–4' tall × 3–10' wide
Disease Resistance: Excellent
Rebloom: Excellent
Garden Uses: Flowerbeds, cut flowers, groupings, small climber, own-root, pollinators

MEMORIAL DAY

Hybrid Tea, 2001

Perfume lovers, take note: this is a rose you can smell from several feet away on a warm, humid day. In fact, this was my initial experience with 'Memorial Day'. With thousands of different pink roses available today, 'Memorial Day' is a standout due to the fragrance alone.

At a glance, 'Memorial Day' seems interchangeable with 'Belinda's Dream': both are upright, leafy shrubs sprinkled with plump reddish buds that unfurl into large pink flowers. On closer inspection, 'Memorial Day' is more of a silvery orchid pink than the carnation pink of 'Belinda's Dream' and has attractively scalloped petal edges. The blooms also develop a cabbage-like, antique appearance as they age. 'Memorial Day's disease resistance is not as strong as 'Belinda's Dream'—but, admittedly, few modern roses are.

So where does 'Memorial Day' gain the upper hand? The answer is in the fragrance department: these flowers are just *oozing* with an overpowering, sharp old-rose incense that has few rivals among pink hybrid teas, although 'Beverly' comes close. Incidentally, the dark pink of 'Beverly' mingles wonderfully with the light pink of 'Memorial Day', as both are cool tones devoid of yellow shading. Place these two side by side in the garden for an overpowering fragrance smorgasbord.

Hybridizer: Tom Carruth
Culture: Easy
Availability: Wide
Fragrance: Powerful old rose
Average Size: 5–6' tall × 4–6' wide
Disease Resistance: Good
Rebloom: Good
Garden Uses: Flowerbeds, cut flowers, groupings

MISTER LINCOLN

Hybrid Tea, 1964

'Mister Lincoln' was once described by *Sunset* magazine as one of the most universally adaptable red roses to grow in any part of the United States. South Florida is no exception; this is a wonderful hybrid tea for our area and still going strong after 60 years in cultivation. Although prone to blackspot, 'Mister Lincoln' grows so vigorously that infected leaves are quickly replaced.

Dark, reddish-black buds with long sepals open into large, high-centered, blood-red flowers emitting an overwhelming damask fragrance. Petals are thick and substantive with a sensuous, velvety quality to them. Flowering stems may be 18" long or more—this is definitely a bouquet rose par excellence.

'Mister Lincoln' forms a very tall (6–7' is typical), stiffly upright shrub with beefy canes studded in squat, triangular thorns. The large leaves are a matte dark green, proportionate to the hefty plant.

This was one of the first roses I ever grew as a teenager in the mid-1990s, and its performance in South Florida has been remarkably similar to that in my Maryland garden. In both regions the plant quickly grows to 6' tall, decks itself out with big flowers, and develops an annual case of blackspot. Summer heat often causes the red color to lighten significantly, but it's worth tolerating for the lusciously sultry winter blooms—which really are magnificent, no matter where in the country you garden.

Hybridizer: Swim & Weeks
Culture: Easy
Availability: Wide
Fragrance: Outstanding damask
Average Size: 6–7' tall × 4–5' wide
Disease Resistance: Fair
Rebloom: Good
Garden Uses: Flowerbeds, cut flowers, groupings

MOSER PINK STRIPED

Tea, date unknown

Striped roses have gone in and out of fashion since the Renaissance, when the first documented cultivar, 'Rosa Mundi', became available to European gardeners in the 1500s. Many striped roses are garish in their coloration, but 'Moser Pink Striped' is done up in subtle elegance—a classic example of "less is more." This variety may take over a year to settle into the garden before producing strong growth, so have patience.

Conical buds gracefully open up into loose, semidouble, deeply cupped blooms of dawn pink irregularly striped and stippled in deep rose. The petals roll back gracefully like gentle ocean waves, which highlights the striping effect by giving it a multidimensional quality. Mature flowers display a golden glow in their nether regions that plays well with the warm pink base color.

'Moser Pink Striped' is one of the smaller-growing tea roses and works well for gardens tight on space. The plant actually grows more like a modern floribunda than a tea rose, with thick, upright canes. Handsome, large, matte green leaves show good overall blackspot resistance.

Although listed as an unscented rose, 'Moser Pink Striped' has always emitted a fairly strong sweet-tea fragrance for me—never dramatic but always pleasant, like the flowers themselves. Use this one to complement other varieties; the bicolored blooms play well with many red, pink, and white roses in the garden.

Hybridizer: Unknown
Culture: Easy
Availability: Moderate
Fragrance: Strong tea
Average Size: 4–5' tall × 4' wide
Disease Resistance: Good
Rebloom: Good
Garden Uses: Flowerbeds, cut flowers, groupings, own-root

MOTHER OF PEARL

Grandiflora, 2007

'Mother of Pearl' is not yet widely available on 'Fortuniana' rootstock, but I expect that to change as more gardeners experience this variety's awesomeness and consumer demand goes up. Hands down, this is easily the best grandiflora I've ever grown! If you can find a 'Fortuniana'-grafted plant, definitely get it: this rose blooms like there's no tomorrow.

'Mother of Pearl' is a real flower factory when she gets going, most likely because the floriferous 'Carefree Wonder' is one of her parents. Big, forked, upright sprays of chiseled buds slowly spiral open into large, lightly scented, hybrid tea-shaped blooms splendid for cutting. Their color is a handsome two-tone apricot: pale seashell on top, deep peach on the back. From a distance, the flowers look like bigger, more intensely saturated versions of 'Safrano'. The large leaves are bright glossy green with reasonable blackspot resistance; the shrub itself is upright and prickly, typical of the grandifloras.

I am constantly amazed by how heavy-blooming 'Mother of Pearl' is. Both young nursery plants and established garden shrubs cover themselves in flowers over and over. Apricot-colored roses like 'Mother of Pearl' also harmonize well with many other garden flowers, especially bright tropical plants. Try several in a large mass alongside variegated shell ginger and scarlet pentas for a warm-hued display overflowing with color all year long.

Hybridizer: Alain Meilland
Culture: Easy
Availability: Moderate
Fragrance: Light, rosy
Average Size: 5–6' tall × 4–5' wide
Disease Resistance: Good
Rebloom: Excellent
Garden Uses: Flowerbeds, cut flowers, groupings

MRS. B. R. CANT

Tea, 1901

'Mrs. B. R. Cant' easily makes my list of the ten best roses for gardening in South Florida. In fact, this rose would be worth growing even if it never flowered: the whole shrub is decked out in beautiful slate-green leaves, silvery underneath, that laugh in the face of disease. To grow this rose is to be reminded of what truly satisfying gardening is really all about.

Long, sculpted buds with beautiful sepals open up into big, full, shallow-cupped blooms of perfect antique formation, with large outer petals cradling a gorgeous rosette of smaller inner petals. Blooms appear as an even shade of deep pink from a distance, but up close you'll get a kaleidoscope of tones: blush in the center, lilac in the guard petals, and subtle brick-red tints throughout. Colors will vary by season but are usually darker in cool weather, lighter in summertime. The earthy tea fragrance is clean and sharp.

'Mrs. B. R. Cant' takes several years to grow to its ultimate height of around 7' or so but will pump out flowers nonstop as it grows. The shrub typically produces a massive flower flush for a month or so, then settles down for a few weeks before starting another flush—and it will repeat this cycle for its entire lifetime in your garden! Not a bad deal.

This rose was named for the wife of the hybridizer, who owned and operated a rose breeding nursery in England during the late 1800s; after his death, his sons continued the family business well into the 1900s.

Hybridizer: Benjamin R. Cant
Culture: Easy
Availability: Wide
Fragrance: Strong earthy tea
Average Size: 6–8' tall × 6–8' wide
Disease Resistance: Excellent
Rebloom: Excellent
Garden Uses: Flowerbeds, cut flowers, groupings, hedge, own-root

MUNSTEAD WOOD

Shrub (David Austin), 2010

My trial plants of 'Munstead Wood' were very open and awkward at first, with sparse, angular canes. It was only after about two years that new growth filled in to create full, rounded shrubs. Planting this variety in groups is a must, both to compensate for sparse young plants and to provide enough flowers for cutting.

Trust me on the latter—'Munstead Wood' is a sultry, sensuous, superb cut flower. The beautifully symmetrical, very full petals look as if cut from red velvet. They are quartered and swirled in the style of the best antique roses, assuming a flattened, saucer-like shape as they age. A tapestry of highlights—magenta, burgundy, and purplish black—gives the blooms incredible gradients of texture and color.

The decadent fragrance is a strong blend of old rose and ripe fruit, perfectly suited to the romantic flower color and shape. Combined with the petals' opulent, velvety texture, it is almost an overload to the senses. Aubergine-tinted new growth matures to dark glossy green with good disease resistance. The canes are viciously spiny, however, so be careful when tending them.

This variety is named for the estate of Gertrude Jekyll, the Victorian garden designer who revolutionized landscape architecture by raising cottage gardens to a state of heightened elegance and meticulous planning. Munstead Wood was Jekyll's residence as well as her show garden for clients, and a consummate example of her signature style.

Hybridizer: David Austin
Culture: Easy
Availability: Moderate
Fragrance: Powerful old rose/fruit blend
Average Size: 4–5' tall × 4' wide
Disease Resistance: Good
Rebloom: Excellent
Garden Uses: Flowerbeds, cut flowers, groupings

NATCHITOCHES NOISETTE

Noisette, date unknown

"An incredible rose, perfect in every way," is how one gardener describes 'Natchitoches Noisette'. After reading several other glowing reviews, I eagerly secured two plants so I could see for myself what the fuss was about. Sure enough, the fuss is well deserved.

Pronounced "NACK-uh-tish," this cultivar was discovered in an old cemetery in Natchitoches, Louisiana. The original plant had a healthy disposition despite obvious neglect, indicating a good shrub to bring into commerce.

Also sold as 'Morgan Spring', this beauty makes a fluffy, informal mass of willowy canes and pointed, dark green leaves. Raspberry-pink buds in upright, candelabra-like bunches open up into shaggy, rounded to cupped blooms of clear light pink, accented with lemon yellow stamens in their middles. The musky fragrance has a subtle myrrh note, an aroma not usually found in the Noisette class.

'Nachitoches Noisette' somewhat reminds me of 'Heritage'—both are blousy, informal shrubs with light pink blossoms attractive to pollinators. Both are also healthy roses that thrive in partial shade. I planted three 'Nachitoches Noisette' on the east side of our house in Cape Coral where they received full, intense morning sun followed by full, bright afternoon shade. To date, we've all been quite happy with the arrangement.

Hybridizer: Unknown
Culture: Easy
Availability: Moderate
Fragrance: Medium musk/myrrh blend
Average Size: 4–6' tall × 5–6' wide
Disease Resistance: Good
Rebloom: Excellent
Garden Uses: Flowerbeds, cut flowers, groupings, pollinators, partial
  shade, own-root

NACOGDOCHES

Floribunda or Grandiflora, date unknown

As the story goes, the original plant of 'Nacogdoches' was discovered growing under the overhang of an abandoned motel in Nacogdoches, Texas. Several cuttings were grown in the garden of elderly Miss Tillie Jungman; the best specimen was then propagated by Texas A&M and entered into commerce as 'Grandma's Yellow' in honor of Miss Jungman, who died in 2005.

Though 'Grandma's Yellow' is now the official name of this cultivar, most gardeners and retailers still use the name 'Nacogdoches'. Nomenclature aside, this variety is payday for those who love yellow roses—the petals are so glossy and saturated that they look almost artificial. Blooms are high-centered florist-style roses initially, with rolled tips that create a star-like outline. They lose their shapeliness as they age, becoming ruffled, amorphous cups, though their color remains fairly intense right until shattering.

'Nacogdoches' has a decidedly modern habit of growth: thorny, upright canes forming a vase-shaped shrub with flowers hovering above the leaves in loose sprays. The foliage is semiglossy green with a brownish cast. Owing to the thorniness and density, 'Nacogdoches' would work well as a barrier hedge.

Dark yellow roses aren't usually my thing, but I love varieties like 'Nacogdoches' that have a charming backstory. Rags-to-riches stories like this one have an allure that penetrates far deeper than mere floral aesthetics do—and that, to me, is definitely worthy of propagation, literally and metaphorically.

Discoverer: Tillie Jungman
Culture: Easy
Availability: Wide
Fragrance: None
Average Size: 5–6' tall × 4–6' wide
Disease Resistance: Excellent
Rebloom: Good
Garden Uses: Flowerbeds, cut flowers, groupings, hedge, Earth-Kind®, own-root, conversation piece

NUR MAHAL

Shrub (Hybrid Musk), 1923

The hybrid musks all make wonderful landscape plants because of their head-to-toe elegance, and 'Nur Mahal' is another great example of that refinement. Named for the wife of Emperor Jahangir, one of the most powerful rulers of India in the 1600s, this rose is exquisitely beautiful in all parts—the arching canes, the beautifully crafted leaves, and the large, cascading trusses of blooms.

In South Florida, 'Nur Mahal' forms a tall, moderately prickly, arching shrub in the 8–12' height range. The foliage is perhaps the loveliest of any rose: large, rounded, wavy-textured leaflets of a beautiful blue green with burgundy shading and a silvery reverse. Each leaflet is folded downward along the midrib and has a drooping tip, creating an enchanting weeping effect.

Branched clusters of pointed buds with foliated sepals open up into ruffled, cherry-red, semidouble blooms that have the same undulating texture as the leaves. Their musky fragrance is rich and sweet. Bees and other pollinators eagerly flock to these blossoms.

Like most hybrid musks, 'Nur Mahal' is really a climber at heart. This rose works well as an arch or obelisk subject, where the weeping flower clusters can best be shown off. Position 'Nur Mahal' near a patio or garden pathway, so that you and your guests can close your eyes, inhale the perfume, and be momentarily transported back in time to the days of the Mughal emperors.

Hybridizer: Rev. Joseph Hardwick Pemberton
Culture: Easy
Availability: Wide
Fragrance: Strong, sweet musk
Average Size: 8–12' tall × 4–8' wide
Disease Resistance: Good
Rebloom: Excellent
Garden Uses: Medium climber, own-root, light shade, specimen, pollinators

OUR LADY OF GUADALUPE

Floribunda, 2000

My first impression of 'Our Lady of Guadalupe' was soured by arrogance on my part: I saw a nursery specimen, sighed, and typed the headline "Just Another Pink Rose" in my mind. Over time, however, I've seen reasons to make a much-needed attitude adjustment.

By far the biggest reason is the prolific bloom. 'Our Lady of Guadalupe' flowers constantly, even in midsummer, throwing out branching bloom clusters over and over again. Each neon pink bud develops into a hybrid tea-shaped flower of soft pink with a darker center. Mature blooms are ruffled and blousy, exposing brown stamens (but not unattractively so).

In many ways, this rose reminds me of a smaller 'Belinda's Dream'—both pump out flowers nonstop in South Florida. 'Our Lady's foliage isn't as bulletproof as 'Belinda's Dream' but still puts on a respectable show, with dark, pointed leaflets reminiscent of many China roses. The shrub is dense and upright and would work well as a low hedge in a sunny area.

'Our Lady of Guadalupe' honors the Mexican title for the Blessed Virgin Mary, associated with the iconic image of Mary—head bent, eyes closed, hands clasped in prayer—in the eponymous basilica in Mexico City. A portion of sales from this rose goes to the Hispanic College Fund, a charity established between the breeder and the United Farm Workers of America.

Hybridizer: Dr. Keith W. Zary
Culture: Easy
Availability: Wide
Fragrance: Moderate, sweet
Average Size: 4–5' tall × 3–4' wide
Disease Resistance: Good
Rebloom: Excellent
Garden Uses: Flowerbeds, cut flowers, groupings, hedge, containers

PENELOPE

Shrub (Hybrid Musk), 1924

This buff beauty was named for the venerated heroine of Greek mythology. Penelope, Queen of Ithaca, was the unbreakable wife of the legendary hero Odysseus. According to legend, she faithfully waited 20 years for Odysseus to return from the Trojan War, staving off violent home invaders all the while— talk about devotion!

Just like its mythical namesake, 'Penelope' mixes equal parts beauty, toughness, and dependability. Terminal clusters of pointed, shell-pink buds open into fragrant, open-faced, semidouble blooms of warm buff with pink shading. The numerous thorny, ropey canes form a hefty, shaggy shrub that can be trained as a climber in South Florida. Stems are blanketed in large, forest-green leaves with a handsome quilted texture. Disease resistance is good on established plants.

This is another rose whose soft tones play well with—and help to tone down—some of our more intensely hued tropical plants. Try 'Penelope' bracketed with clumps of red and yellow 'Jacquinii' heliconias: the feminine flowers weaving in and out of the bold heliconia leaves will be a twenty-first-century metaphor for the mythical queen dodging the aggressive suitors who chased her for two decades.

Hybridizer: Rev. Joseph Hardwick Pemberton
Culture: Easy
Availability: Wide
Fragrance: Strong, sweet musk
Average Size: 6–12' tall × 8–12' wide
Disease Resistance: Good
Rebloom: Excellent
Garden Uses: Medium climber, cut flowers, groupings, own-root,
    partial shade

PERLE D'OR

Polyantha, 1875

As I've delved into cottage gardening in South Florida, I've gotten more into roses with a rustic charm about them—and 'Perle d'Or' is nothing if not rustic. The warm color gradient plays well with many other garden flowers; for anyone trying to create an English-style South Florida garden, this one's a must-have.

A dense, spreading shrub, 'Perle d'Or' produces flowers in large, multi-branched clusters held above the foliage. Small hybrid tea-shaped buds open into a fluffy mass of slender, strap-like petals that reflex into pompons. Mature flowers look more like chrysanthemums or zinnias than roses. Established plants are virtually everblooming, sending up a new flower flush right after the previous one finishes and lending the plant great value for landscaping. Polished mahogany new growth ages to medium green, semiglossy leaves with strong disease resistance.

In the cool of winter and spring, 'Perle d'Or's buds are a warm orangey apricot and open up into a soft peach color. Hot weather causes the flowers to lighten to seashell pink fading to white in the outermost petals. Regardless of season, they always emit a sweet peppery fragrance, so try to site 'Perle d'Or' close to a patio or walkway.

Hybridizer: Joseph Rambaux
Culture: Easy
Availability: Wide
Fragrance: Strong, sweet peppery
Average Size: 3–5' tall × 4–6' wide
Disease Resistance: Excellent
Rebloom: Excellent
Garden Uses: Flowerbeds, cut flowers, groupings, containers,
    Earth-Kind®, own-root

PING DONG YUE JI

China or Tea, 1930

'Ping Dong Yue Ji' is my favorite of the "Asian Mystery" roses, as I call them—a handful of uncommon roses with obscure Chinese origins. This variety may occasionally be listed by some retailers as 'Mother Dudley.'

'Ping Dong Yue Ji' starts out as pointed buds that develop into cupped flowers of opalescent dawn pink with darker centers and a lovely honeysuckle fragrance. Mature blooms flatten into pompons; cool weather results in bigger flowers with faint quartering and knotted petaloids in their centers. The upright shrub has healthy leaves of medium green with red-tinted rachises.

While there is definitely no shortage of pink roses out there, 'Ping Dong Yue Ji' has one unusual leg up over the competition: the shrub's panicles (branched flowering stems) are perhaps the most elegant of any rose—broadly swirled and curled like an Alphonse Mucha whiplash. The allusion to artwork is fitting; one gardener eloquently compared her plant to a paintbrush stroking a smooth curve.

Beautiful floral nuances like these have inspired artists since time immemorial. Plant 'Ping Dong Yue Ji' in a prominent spot in your garden: once it matures, the gracefully curving stems will wave about like a living Art Nouveau painting, all for your own private, personal enjoyment.

Discoverer: Kun Wang
Culture: Easy
Availability: Limited
Fragrance: Strong honeysuckle
Average Size: 4–5' tall × 4' wide
Disease Resistance: Excellent
Rebloom: Excellent
Garden Uses: Flowerbeds, cut flowers, groupings, own-root

POPE JOHN PAUL II

Hybrid Tea, 2006

Every gardener should grow at least one white hybrid tea at some point in their lifetime, and here's why: after a particularly bad day, it is ineffably soul-refreshing to step into the garden and see a single, magnificent rose of clear, pristine beauty to help wash away all that bad energy.

With so many white hybrid teas to choose from, which one is best for our corner of America? My vote goes to 'Pope John Paul II' without even a speck of hesitation.

'PJP', as this rose is often abbreviated, is splendid enough to win over even the stoniest of anti-hybrid tea hearts. Large, chiseled buds with elaborate sepals are lime green at first but slowly expand into glorious, massive, crystal-white roses blessed with a penetrating spicy perfume. Long stems render the flowers perfect for cutting. The shrub is one of the more graceful hybrid teas, symmetrical and well cloaked in glossy, dark green leaves—the perfect backdrop for these immaculate flowers. Established plants are never out of bloom.

My favorite way to use 'PJP' is in an all-white-and-silver garden. Partner these flawless white blooms with a sweet almond bush, white pentas, and some gray-leaved harmonizers like dusty miller, Parson's junipers, and the always-dramatic silver alcantarea bromeliad (*Alcantarea odorata*).

Hybridizer: Dr. Keith W. Zary
Culture: Easy
Availability: Wide
Fragrance: Strong citrus/jasmine blend
Average Size: 5–6' tall × 4' wide
Disease Resistance: Good
Rebloom: Excellent
Garden Uses: Flowerbeds, cut flowers, groupings

POSEIDON

Floribunda, 2004

Also listed as 'Novalis', 'Poseidon' has been described as a rose that does poorly in hot climates, so I had low expectations for my lone trial plant. But it surprised me with such a knockout performance that I quickly bought three more, to create a beautiful grouping at the end of a bed in my Oakland Park garden.

'Poseidon' is uncharacteristically tall for a floribunda, with moderately thorny canes easily reaching 6–7' tall. The large leaves are a dark blue green that perfectly complements the flower color. As with all Kordes roses, this is a healthy variety that rarely needs spraying to stay leafy.

Large buds, usually in upright clusters, are kidney bean red streaked with white at first. These slowly expand into truly magnificent, extremely full and rounded flowers of rich, saturated lavender. The outer petals fade to pewter gray while the lavender hues get deeper and darker toward each flower's center—an amazing display of cool tones that greatly temper all the warm colors common in South Florida gardens. Each petal has a recurved, pointed tip that, combined with the flowers' globular silhouette, results in a charming "old meets new" look not seen in many other roses.

'Poseidon's cool season blooms are often 5" or more across, so heavy that they nod on the canes. Flowers almost always occur on long, cutting-length stems—so if you include 'Poseidon' in your garden, be sure to keep clean vases at the ready.

Hybridizer: Tim Hermann Kordes
Culture: Easy
Availability: Moderate
Fragrance: Medium, rosy
Average Size: 6–7' tall × 3–4' wide
Disease Resistance: Excellent
Rebloom: Excellent
Garden Uses: Flowerbeds, cut flowers, groupings

PRINCESS CHARLENE DE MONACO®

Hybrid Tea, 2012

'Princess Charlene de Monaco' is so antique looking that it's easy to mistake it for a David Austin creation. Such was my initial encounter: I found an unlabeled nursery plant and spent the next week repeatedly asking the David Austin nursery in England to help identify it. They insisted it wasn't one of theirs, while I was positive it was. Finally, a fellow gardener posted a picture of this variety on Instagram, and the mystery was solved—with me eating a big piece of humble pie in the process.

Pink buds with warm yellow shading gently expand into wonderfully large, deliciously fragrant, wavy-textured blooms with scalloped petals crimped and folded like pomegranate blossoms. They are done up in a watercolor of light salmon pink and peach fading to white in the outer petals. The color effect is like the rising sun casting its luminosity onto nearby clouds, thrilling and calming all at once.

Although a hybrid tea, this variety's long, sinuous canes work best trained horizontally as a climber in South Florida; doing this will maximize bloom production by initiating lateral flower buds. The rounded, glossy leaflets are an unusually bright blue green and have reasonable disease resistance.

Born in Zimbabwe in 1978, Charlene Lynette Wittstock rose to fame as an Olympic swimmer in the 1990s and 2000s. In 2010, she became engaged to Prince Albert II of Monaco, marrying him in an opulent ceremony the following year; since then, Charlene has devoted much of her time fundraising for the Special Olympics and HIV/AIDS charities in Africa.

Hybridizer: Alain Meilland
Culture: Easy
Availability: Wide
Fragrance: Strong fruit/allspice blend
Average Size: 7–9' tall × 4–5' wide
Disease Resistance: Good
Rebloom: Good
Garden Uses: Small climber, cut flowers

PROSPERITY

Shrub (Hybrid Musk), 1919

At first, 'Prosperity' was a colossal letdown for me. Because it's frequently described as a good, disease-resistant rose for partial shade, I placed my trial plant near a crape myrtle tree—where it was promptly and completely defoliated by blackspot. Not exactly the iron-clad plant touted by nurseries.

When healthy and well grown, however, this is a spectacular climber. Like most hybrid musks, 'Prosperity' produces massive trusses of 20 or more blooms. Half-opened buds are flushed with pink but open up a pure snowy white. The small, dense flowers are so numerous that the branches will gracefully weep under their weight; a mature plant cascading with flowers is a splendid sight in the garden. Bees seem to enjoy these blossoms despite how double they are.

'Prosperity' forms an arching mound of long, pliable canes best trained over a large garden structure—this is a *huge* climber, so give it plenty of room to romp. New growth is bright red, maturing to holly-shaped leaflets of very glossy dark green. Young stems have a unique zigzag shape.

About a year after my first attempt with 'Prosperity', I planted a new specimen in a full sun location near our patio. Without any overhead shade, this one grew rapidly and exhibited the disease resistance described by retailers. Lesson learned: if you want 'Prosperity' to live up to its name, give this rose as much sun as possible.

Hybridizer: Rev. Joseph Hardwick Pemberton
Culture: Easy
Availability: Wide
Fragrance: Light, musky
Average Size: 15–25' tall × 10–20' wide
Disease Resistance: Good
Rebloom: Excellent
Garden Uses: Large climber, pollinators

PUERTO RICO

Tea, date unknown

I've struggled with math ever since I was little. Fortunately, roses like 'Puerto Rico' teach all the math that a gardener need ever possess. It's a simple equation, really: gorgeous blooms + wonderful fragrance × several years of performance = one giant heap of delight. Take that, calculus!

A tea rose originally found on the eponymous island and brought to the United States shortly thereafter, 'Puerto Rico' forms a vase-shaped shrub composed of stiffly ascending canes. The whole plant is draped with large, clean leaves of bright olive green.

The lovely flowers are remarkably modern looking for a tea rose: big, high-centered blooms of blush white with darker centers that emerge from large, chiseled buds. Flowers are mostly in upward-pointing clusters; their perfume is strong, sweet, and fruity; and the repeat bloom on established shrubs is truly outstanding. The large winter blooms are especially striking in their trifecta of color, form, and scent.

Rose enthusiasts argue about the exact origins of this rose: some say it actually hails from Bermuda and is properly named 'Maitland White'. Either way, this rose most likely emerged from a tropical Atlantic island, hence its adaptability to South Florida's growing conditions.

Discoverer: José Marrero
Culture: Easy
Availability: Moderate
Fragrance: Strong, fruity
Average Size: 6' tall × 4–5' wide
Disease Resistance: Excellent
Rebloom: Excellent
Garden Uses: Flowerbeds, cut flowers, groupings, own-root

QUIETNESS

Shrub, 2003

Dr. Griffith Buck, a horticulture professor at the University of Iowa, made it his mission to develop a line of roses that could survive freezing Iowa winters without protection. An unintentional side effect of his meticulous breeding program is that many of his roses grow just as well in hot climates as they do in cold climates, simply because their pedigree is so hearty.

'Quietness' is one such heat-tolerant "Buck" rose, as they're called. Although classed as a shrub, the plant grows more like a contemporary hybrid tea, with thick canes forming a very upright, vase-shaped plant. The foliage is a glossy medium green.

Conical buds, either singly or in small clusters, erupt into big, high-centered blooms of tender light pink blushing darker toward their centers. The lovely blooms are produced on long stems good for cutting and give off a delectable, strong aroma. Flowers take on a shaggy appearance as they age, with the petal edges often reflexing into pointed tips.

'Quietness' seems to grow well as an own-root plant in South Florida: one of my friends has had one in her Miami garden for several years now without any issues. Plants grafted on 'Fortuniana', of course, are a safer bet. Use 'Quietness' toward the back of a bed with some 'Nora Grant' ixoras for a beautiful garden tapestry of light and dark pinks.

Hybridizer: Dr. Griffith Buck
Culture: Easy
Availability: Moderate
Fragrance: Delicious, strong, and sweet
Average Size: 6–8' tall × 5–7' wide
Disease Resistance: Good
Rebloom: Good
Garden Uses: Flowerbeds, cut flowers, groupings, own-root

RED EDEN™

Large-Flowered Climber, 2004

A friend in Vietnam described 'Red Eden' as thriving in her sweltering tropical garden—my first clue that this rose is well suited to South Florida. If you're looking for another red climber besides the ubiquitous 'Don Juan', give this one a try.

Globular crimson buds with charcoal shading are so round that they look almost like berries. These open into equally plump, incurved rosettes of the same rich crimson. Petals are arranged in a truly stunning quartered formation, like the roses in a seventeenth-century Dutch painting. Summertime flowers are subject to balling, but the blooms are splendid the rest of the year. The large leaves are a very dramatic glossy jade green.

'Red Eden's fragrance is the most variable of any rose I've ever experienced. On cool days I can detect nothing, no matter how hard I try. (I can only imagine what the neighbors think when they see a large tattooed man sniffing a rose with the temerity of a police dog sniffing for contraband.) But on hot days, I get a blast of tangy damask perfume coming from deep within each flower.

For those who love roses for cutting, 'Red Eden' has the longest-lasting blooms of any rose I've ever grown in over 25 years. Their average vase life is ten days, and I once had a spray of blossoms that lasted for over two weeks—I simply kept changing the vase water every morning.

Hybridizer: Alain Meilland
Culture: Easy
Availability: Limited
Fragrance: Variable: nonexistent to medium damask
Average Size: 10–12' tall × 4–6' wide
Disease Resistance: Fair
Rebloom: Excellent
Garden Uses: Medium climber, cut flowers

ROSE DE RESCHT

Portland or Damask Perpetual, date unknown

This dainty rose originated near the Iranian town of Rescht, where it was discovered by English plant collector Nancy Lindsay in 1945. Beyond that, it's a bit of a mystery. Some say 'Rose de Rescht' is an ancient damask perpetual; others insist it's a Portland, bred in France in the late 1700s, then brought to Iran in the early 1800s.

While the true origins may never be known, this is nevertheless a delightful little charmer for South Florida. 'Rose de Rescht' is one of the most compact roses for our gardens, seldom more than 3' tall or wide. The soft green foliage comes right up to the base of the flowers—what renowned British rosarian Graham Stuart Thomas called a "shoulder of leaves."

Dark red, fat little buds with ornate sepals expand into small rosettes packed with petals in classic antique formation. They are bright magenta with crimson to purplish shading. But more than their intense color, the penetrating fragrance is the real showstopper here. 'Rose de Rescht' emits a piercing perfume that smells just like fresh strawberry pie—sweet, strong, and fruity. Plant this one in groups of three or more, so you can enjoy the aroma both indoors and out.

The rebloom is outstanding from fall through late spring, with a few scattered flowers in summer. 'Rose de Rescht' also does well in afternoon shade, so consider this one for part-shade positions where other roses struggle.

Discoverer: Nancy Lindsay
Culture: Easy
Availability: Wide
Fragrance: Powerful strawberry/old rose blend
Average Size: 3–4' tall × 3–4' wide
Disease Resistance: Fair
Rebloom: Good
Garden Uses: Flowerbeds, cut flowers, groupings, own-root, containers, partial shade

ROSETTE DELIZY

Tea, 1922

Of all my 100 rose entries, 'Rosette Delizy' endured the most rewrites prior to publication. The reason why is simple: I struggled to find words that could do proper justice to such a beautiful living thing.

A flower that simultaneously exudes both polished poise and simple cheerfulness is hard to summarize in just one page—but, that is 'Rosette Delizy'. The shrub is so handsome that it almost takes your breath away: dark mahogany stems draped in glossy green leaves with red petioles, a flawless backdrop for the brilliant blooms.

Flowers are heavily produced all year long and go through several transformations in color and shape as they age. The pointed buds are light red with chartreuse shading initially, with petal tips rolled back into spirals. Half-opened flowers are high-centered cups the color of lemon curd with cherry pink towards the petal tips. Finally, the mature bloom is a full and fluffy rosette (hence the name) of ochre-yellow inner petals snuggled inside two or three rows of larger, soft pink outer petals.

Along with 'Marinette', 'Rosette Delizy' is a joyous flower that instantly puts a smile on your face and is a wonderful means of adding a splash of soft, warm pastels to the garden. Give this rose equally soft-yet-warm companions: 'Coral Nymph' salvia and 'Orange Marmalade' crossandra both look splendid in combination.

Hybridizer: Clément Nabonnand
Culture: Easy
Availability: Moderate
Fragrance: Medium tea
Average Size: 4' tall × 4–5' wide
Disease Resistance: Excellent
Rebloom: Excellent
Garden Uses: Flowerbeds, cut flowers, groupings, own-root

SAFRANO

Tea, 1839

'Safrano' grows so well in South Florida that it's hard to not include one in every garden that I design. One of the few truly beige flowers available, the neutral petal color associates effortlessly with almost all others in a planting scheme. If roses had taglines, "plays well with others" would be 'Safrano's.

A more restrained tea rose here, 'Safrano' stays around 4' to 5' in height and spread. New growth is gorgeous plum purple, maturing to semiglossy dark green; both hues perfectly complement the flower color. Half-open buds, long and sculpted, are rich apricot ivory with an initial salmon glow that pales to soft beige as the blooms age. The blooms flatten out considerably before shattering. Though not as poised as the mature flowers of other roses, they nevertheless have a humble charm about them.

A primrose yellow sport, 'Isabella Sprunt', discovered in 1855, is identical to 'Safrano' in every way except color. Both make equally good South Florida roses.

This is a rose you need never spray, even when blackspot is at its worst. And 'Safrano' blooms so abundantly—I daresay excessively—that this alone is reason enough to plant one. Take advantage of the petals' muted colors by giving 'Safrano' a gaudy assortment of striped bromeliads as a foreground planting.

Hybridizer: Beauregard
Culture: Easy
Availability: Wide
Fragrance: Musky tea/fruit blend
Average Size: 4–5' tall × 4–5' wide
Disease Resistance: Excellent
Rebloom: Excellent
Garden Uses: Flowerbeds, cut flowers, groupings, own-root,
    pollinators

SAI ZHAO JUN

China, date unknown

'Sai Zhao Jun' is a rose that I initially overlooked but now go out of my way to dote on lovingly. This cultivar has a quirky beauty all its own, coupled with a tidy habit of growth and good health. The name is pronounced "SIGH jao junn."

The flowers of 'Sai Zhao Jun' are chameleonlike in their ability to change colors throughout the year. Midsummer blooms are typically a deep, cool pink washing lighter in the outer petals; winter flowers are a mix of white and peachy apricot with fuchsia tracing on their tips.

The one constant seems to be the peculiar, angular petals. They are rhomboidal to quill shaped, irregularly crimped, asymmetrically arranged—yet they somehow come together to form an evenly balanced flower. To me, the blooms embody the Eastern philosophy of wabi-sabi, the beauty inherent in nature's imperfections.

Unlike many other China roses in South Florida, 'Sai Zhao Jun' remains a manageable shrub around 4' tall and wide. Mature plants produce incredible flushes of flowers held upright in airy, branched clusters. The pale winter flowers remind me of the popular David Austin rose 'Sharifa Asma', but on a much healthier, easier-to-grow plant.

Hybridizer: Unknown
Culture: Easy
Availability: Limited
Fragrance: Strong, sweet tea
Average Size: 4–5' tall × 4' wide
Disease Resistance: Good
Rebloom: Excellent
Garden Uses: Flowerbeds, cut flowers, groupings, own-root

SCENTIMENTAL™

Floribunda, 1997

'Scentimental' is one of the most popular creations from American breeder Tom Carruth—and the first striped rose ever to win the annual All-America Rose Selections (AARS) award. Many striped roses have existed since ancient times, but most are once-blooming European roses that do best in cold climates. Luckily for South Floridians, 'Scentimental' blooms all year long here with no winter chill required.

Clear, bright crimson petals are broadly splashed in a sugary white that can sometimes appear light pink from a distance. The color effect is instantly evocative of a bowl of peppermint candies at Christmastime. Along with their sweet damask fragrance, these flowers are perfect for a holiday table arrangement.

The 3–4" blooms are deeply cupped and semidouble to fully double, depending on weather. Personally, I find both situations equally attractive— when the flowers are less double, 'Scentimental' shows off a cheerful mass of yellow stamens.

Expect 'Scentimental' to form a typically floribunda-ish plant: upright and stiff to around 4' or so, with puckered leaflets of dark olive green shaded red near their margins. Disease resistance is average at best; 'Scentimental' isn't as healthy as 'Madame Driout' or 'Moser Pink Striped', but the striping effect is infinitely more dramatic. Especially around the winter holidays, 'Scentimental' makes for a gorgeous addition to the South Florida garden.

Hybridizer: Tom Carruth
Culture: Easy
Availability: Wide
Fragrance: Moderate damask
Average Size: 4–5' tall × 3–4' wide
Disease Resistance: Fair
Rebloom: Excellent
Garden Uses: Flowerbeds, cut flowers, groupings, conversation piece

SETINA

Bourbon/China, 1879

What an underappreciated beauty 'Setina' has proven to be. A climbing sport of a popular Bourbon called 'Hermosa', 'Setina' is tough as nails, just like the parent plant. I once transplanted a specimen in the middle of August—an act that would easily kill a more delicate rose. But 'Setina' wasn't fazed in the least, and the plant established itself as if it had been transplanted in January. It can't be overemphasized: tough as nails.

'Setina' forms a sizable climber, with long, ropey canes covered in dark green leaves and the hooked thorns typical of Bourbon/China roses. These prickles will easily do damage to human flesh, so exercise caution when working around them.

Flowers start out as cherry-pink buds held on short axillary stalks. These unravel into cupped, semidouble blooms of rich pink suffused with lilac. Petal edges gently roll back, giving a cheerful cottage garden feel to the blooms. Reports of 'Setina's fragrance vary widely, but to my nose it has a moderate tea scent.

South Florida is blessed with a wide range of vining and climbing plants: Confederate jasmine, blue sky vine, passion flower, bougainvillea. All are lovely but tend to quickly overwhelm their spaces in our warm climate. Climbing roses like 'Setina', on the other hand, are often easier to keep within bounds and should be given more consideration for situations where a climbing flower is desired.

Hybridizer: Peter Henderson
Culture: Easy
Availability: Wide
Fragrance: Medium tea
Average Size: 15' tall × 8–10' wide
Disease Resistance: Excellent
Rebloom: Excellent
Garden Uses: Tall climber, cut flowers, own-root

SHUI MEI REN

China or Tea, date unknown

'Shui Mei Ren' (sometimes also spelled 'Sui Mei Ren') is for people who want a piece of living history in their gardens. The flowers are lovely enough, but it's this variety's backstory that makes for an exciting conversation piece in the garden.

According to the current lore, 'Shui Mei Ren' was collected from the Huai'an Rose Garden in Jiangsu, China. The staff there say that the original specimen dates back to the Song Dynasty, which means that 'Shui Mei Ren' was first bred between 960 and 1279 CE—which, if true, makes this rose one of the oldest varieties in existence today. Only a handful of others, primarily from Europe, are as old or older.

'Shui Mei Ren' blooms heavily with lovely flowers so full of quill-shaped petals that they appear more like dahlias or chrysanthemums at first. Their apricot color is unusual for a China and probably indicates some influence from a tea rose ancestor. Flowers are usually in sprays of four. Opinions vary on the fragrance; to me, it's a moderately strong, earthy tea scent. The foliage is highly unusual for a China rose: large, rounded leaflets of rich kelly green that look curiously modern to me.

This is a unique rose that should be more widely planted in South Florida simply because of how well it tackles humid heat. 'Shui Mei Ren' is Mandarin for "Sleeping Beauty." The name is pronounced "SCHWAY may wren."

Discoverer: Dr. Yoshihiro Oeda
Culture: Easy
Availability: Moderate
Fragrance: Medium tea
Average Size: 4' tall × 3–4' wide
Disease Resistance: Good
Rebloom: Good
Garden Uses: Flowerbeds, cut flowers, groupings, conversation piece

SOUVENIR DE ST. ANNE'S

Bourbon, 1950

'Souvenir de St. Anne's' is a sport of 'Souvenir de la Malmaison', one of the most famous roses ever bred. Both are excellent South Florida roses, but I prefer 'St. Anne's' because the semidouble flowers don't have 'Malmaison's balling problem. My love of single and semidouble roses has grown exponentially over the years, and this is one of the roses that fueled that love.

Upright sprays of pointed buds unfurl into broadly cupped, slightly-more-than-single roses of the most translucent pale pink imaginable. One gardener compared them to the finest bone china that her grandmother owned—the stuff reserved strictly for special occasions. The blooms' fragrance is a pervasive blend of spicy tea and jasmine, and the repeat bloom is truly endless. Mature plants rarely grow over 3' tall and wide, perfect for containers and small spaces.

'St. Anne's' is not 100 percent disease-proof in South Florida: the medium green foliage does get some blackspot here. Fortunately, the plant replaces diseased leaves so quickly that it comes across as healthy overall. 'St. Anne's' definitely resents both hard pruning and transplanting, however. Avoid moving this rose once it's planted in the garden, and give it only light trimmings to remove spent flowers or crossing branches.

This rose is named for St. Anne's Park in Dublin, Ireland, where it was discovered in 1950, the sole mutation in a large bed of 'Souvenir de la Malmaison'—talk about your luck of the Irish.

Discoverer: H. Tilling & Co.
Culture: Easy
Availability: Wide
Fragrance: Outstanding tea/jasmine blend
Average Size: 3' tall × 3' wide
Disease Resistance: Good
Rebloom: Excellent
Garden Uses: Flowerbeds, cut flowers, groupings, containers, Earth-Kind®, own-root, pollinators

SPICE

Tea, date unknown (possibly 1809)

'Spice' is a must-have for South Florida gardens, flourishing in our humid heat, flowering constantly and abundantly, and exhibiting flawless disease resistance all the while. The sweet-peppery fragrance just makes this fine rose even better.

Also called 'Bermuda Spice' by retailers, this variety forms a dense, twiggy, slow-growing shrub noticeably wider than tall, with soft green leaves and recurved prickles. Sprays of tapered buds are pure white with dark pink streaks at first; these open into small, full, loose-petaled flowers of pale blush that frequently nod horizontally.

A few rosarians believe 'Spice' is really 'Hume's Blush Tea-Scented China', one of the "Four Stud Chinas" from the late 1700s. This foursome revolutionized roses forever by giving their offspring the genes for remontancy, the ability for a rosebush to rebloom after its initial spring flowering wraps up.

Despite the "China" in the name, 'Hume's Blush' is genetically closer to the tea roses. True China roses are descendants of *Rosa chinensis,* while 'Hume's Blush' is descended from *R. gigantea,* a massive climber from the Himalayas that can grow to 30' or more in length. It's hard to imagine a meek, timid-looking rose like 'Spice'/'Hume's Blush' touting the immense *R. gigantea* as a predecessor. But it's really no different than the miniature poodles of today proudly boasting the hulking gray wolf as a distant ancestor. Sometimes truth really is stranger than fiction.

Hybridizer: Unknown (possibly Sir Abraham Hume)
Culture: Easy
Availability: Wide
Fragrance: Strong, sweet, peppery
Average Size: 4' tall × 4–5' wide
Disease Resistance: Excellent
Rebloom: Excellent
Garden Uses: Flowerbeds, cut flowers, groupings, Earth-Kind®,
    own-root, hedge, conversation piece

ST. PATRICK

Hybrid Tea, 1986

Since its debut in the late 1980s, 'St. Patrick' has become an exceedingly popular rose. It is usually available on 'Fortuniana' rootstock, a blessing for those in South Florida who want one (or two, or eight). In the past I've been critical of the flowers' lack of strong green coloration, but over the years 'St. Patrick' has won me over—the many pluses far outweigh this one minus.

With a name like 'St. Patrick', the flower color should be instantly evocative of Ireland—in other words, green. Unfortunately, the only green in this rose occurs very early on, when the buds are a third open. At this stage, petals are pale chartreuse with lime green shading. As they mature, however, the flowers become an even primrose yellow, usually darker in their centers. It's a gorgeous color, but not really green. Occasionally, the open flowers retain some pale green pigmentation in the outermost petals, but this is inconsistent at best.

People buying 'St. Patrick' in hopes of a really green-tinted rose will probably be disappointed. Fortunately, this rose compensates in numerous other ways: the shrub itself is very healthy for a hybrid tea; it doesn't grow overly large in South Florida; and established plants rebloom tirelessly all year long. The wonderfully large and shapely blooms are also very long lasting as cut flowers. If you can accept the flowers as more yellow than green, 'St. Patrick' will make a fine addition to your garden.

Hybridizer: Frank A. Strickland
Culture: Easy
Availability: Wide
Fragrance: Light to none
Average Size: 4–5' tall × 3–4' wide
Disease Resistance: Good
Rebloom: Excellent
Garden Uses: Flowerbeds, cut flowers, groupings, conversation piece

SWEET FRANCES

Shrub, 2007

The parents of 'Sweet Frances' include two excellent, popular roses, 'Heritage' and 'Carefree Beauty'—both of which are strongly fragrant. Sadly, 'Sweet Frances' has no perfume here in South Florida, despite descriptions to the contrary. This could be because rose fragrances are highly regional: a variety that's heavily perfumed in Milwaukee may smell like nothing in Miami.

Fortunately, 'Sweet Frances' makes up elsewhere for its scentlessness. The plant inherited the gracefully arching growth of 'Heritage' and works equally well as either a shrub or a small climber. 'Sweet Frances' also received 'Heritage's floriferousness: flowers, in terminal and axillary clusters of three, bloom heavily even in the heat of summer. The beautifully symmetrical rosettes feature rounded petals arranged around a tight button eye, all done up in light porcelain pink with apricot shading. Blooms typically nod gracefully under their own weight along the canes.

'Sweet Frances' also got a good dose from both parents in the foliage department. The handsome, dark green leaflets are rounded and curled like 'Heritage' and have the good disease resistance of 'Carefree Beauty'. Blackspot can flare up occasionally but is rarely serious enough to warrant a heavy spray program.

This rose is not widely available on 'Fortuniana' yet, but definitely keep a look out for the future. This is a wonderfully heat-tolerant rose, with a truly romantic flower form not seen in many other varieties here.

Hybridizer: Mike Shoup
Culture: Easy
Availability: Limited
Fragrance: Light
Average Size: 6–8' tall × 4–5' wide
Disease Resistance: Good
Rebloom: Excellent
Garden Uses: Flowerbeds, cut flowers, groupings, small climber

TAHITIAN SUNSET

Hybrid Tea, 2006

I have a lot of fondness for 'Tahitian Sunset'. Along with 'Flo Nelson', this is one whose warm color gradient mingles effortlessly with most other garden colors, especially the tropical fare common in South Florida. The incredible fragrance just makes a good thing even better.

The colors of 'Tahitian Sunset' are accurately described by the name, although 'Summer Fruit Salad' would be equally fitting (but far less eloquent). These blooms are a beautiful swirl of tropical fruits: citrus yellow, guava pink, papaya orange. The overall color effect is a warm peachy pink like 'Abraham Darby', with a few buff and magenta highlights thrown in for good measure. Flowers are impressive, large, shapely examples of hybrid tea loveliness and give off a powerful perfume of old rose mixed with fruit and jasmine that you'll want to inhale repeatedly.

'Tahitian Sunset' forms an upright, stalwart, thorny plant decked out in large, dark green leaves with a bronzy tint that nicely complements the flower colors. The foliage has good blackspot resistance as well.

A rose with such a tropical name and coloration deserves equally tropical playmates. Try 'Tahitian Sunset' in a bed with 'Maui Yellow' ixoras, purple New Guinea impatiens, and the spiky, silvery leaves of the Keys thatch palm *(Leucothrinax morrisii)*, one of our smallest—and most beautiful—native palms.

Hybridizer: Dr. Keith W. Zary
Culture: Easy
Availability: Wide
Fragrance: Strong spicy/fruity blend
Average Size: 5–6' tall × 5' wide
Disease Resistance: Good
Rebloom: Good
Garden Uses: Flowerbeds, cut flowers, groupings

TWILIGHT ZONE

Grandiflora, 2012

Along with 'Rose de Rescht', 'Twilight Zone' is one of the best dark-colored roses for morning sun and afternoon shade exposures. An improvement over one of its parents, the purple floribunda 'Ebb Tide', 'Twilight Zone' is a much healthier alternative that still embodies the unique color and heady fragrance of its predecessor.

Upright, candelabra-like clusters of plump, dark red buds with gorgeous feathery sepals open into very full, rounded, shallow-cupped blooms of velvety wine purple. They have an appropriately rich perfume of old rose and cloves. Winter flowers have a sumptuous old-rose appearance that could easily be mistaken for a David Austin rose; summer flowers are open cupped and have fewer petals. The tall, upright plant is remarkably graceful for a grandiflora, draped in handsomely serrated, rounded, dark blue-green leaflets.

This rose tends to be slow growing in my experience, so give it the best care possible. Tons of composted manure and organic fertilizers will make 'Twilight Zone' happy. A healthy, well-tended plant will flower with outstanding generosity: I once counted 15 buds, in various stages of opening, in one opulently massive, long-stemmed cluster.

Like many red and crimson roses here, 'Twilight Zone's burgundy color will lighten significantly in the sweltering heat of midsummer. Adding soil acidifiers can deepen the flower color and may also intensify the blooms' perfume.

Hybridizer: Tom Carruth
Culture: Easy
Availability: Wide
Fragrance: Powerful old rose/clove blend
Average Size: 6–7' tall × 4–5' wide
Disease Resistance: Good
Rebloom: Excellent
Garden Uses: Flowerbeds, cut flowers, groupings, partial shade

VANESSA BELL

Shrub (David Austin), 2017

It's a shame that 'Vanessa Bell' is not more available on 'Fortuniana'. This is one of the most magnificent yellow roses ever created, with a unique, ethereal beauty totally unparalleled in other yellow varieties. And that beauty comes on a healthy, strong-growing, heavy-blooming shrub that basks in South Florida's humid heat. Hopefully more growers will pick this variety up sooner rather than later.

The flowers of 'Vanessa Bell' are like something out of a fairy tale. Long, slender stems, wonderful for cutting, terminate in forked clusters of buds that slowly open into deeply cupped, antique-shaped roses of the softest lemon chiffon imaginable. The outer petals gently fade to almost pure white. Each bloom is blessed with an appropriately fresh scent of sweet tea and citrus that is never too strong—with 'Vanessa Bell', color and fragrance sing together in perfect, graceful harmony.

Along with 'Windermere' and 'Heritage', 'Vanessa Bell' is one of the heaviest-blooming Austin roses for South Florida. In fact, this is one of the heaviest-blooming of *any* rose for South Florida. If you can find one, definitely get it.

Born in 1879, Vanessa Bell (née Stephen) was an accomplished painter in Victorian England. She disliked the standard Victorian "narrative painting" style popular in her time and instead dabbled in postimpressionism and abstraction—both considered highly experimental, even controversial, back then. She frequently designed the book jackets for the works of her sister, writer Virginia Woolf.

Hybridizer: David Austin
Culture: Easy
Availability: Limited
Fragrance: Fresh citrus/tea blend
Average Size: 4–5' tall × 4–5' wide
Disease Resistance: Good
Bloom Frequency: Excellent
Garden Uses: Flowerbeds, cut flowers, groupings

VANITY

Shrub (Hybrid Musk), 1920

With a name like 'Vanity', you would expect an elaborate, very double flower on a high-maintenance plant—the floral equivalent of a haute couture gown on the Paris runways. In actuality, this variety is the polar opposite: the simplest flowers imaginable come atop an easygoing, unfussy shrub. With 'Vanity', you get less haute couture and more casual daywear.

A floppy, shaggy, informal shrub, 'Vanity' produces long canes good for training as a modest climber; this is not an overly thorny rose, so training is fairly user-friendly. Reddish new growth matures to glossy green, downward-curled leaflets with a yellowish tint.

Flowers are produced abundantly throughout the year in South Florida. Pointed buds, usually in cylindrical clusters, open into five-petaled, saucer-shaped flowers of clear deep pink, each anchored with a clump of fuzzy stamens. Cool weather will occasionally encourage a few extra petals, but for most of the year there will be just five broadly overlapping petals serving wild rose realness. A sweet musk fragrance emanates from these blossoms, filling the air on warm days.

'Vanity's single flowers are pollinator magnets. For a backyard brimming with butterflies, use one or two in a large bed along with Mexican sunflower, red firespike, blue porterweed, and a foreground border of yellow butter daisy (*Melampodium divaricatum*).

Hybridizer: Rev. Joseph Hardwick Pemberton
Culture: Easy
Availability: Wide
Fragrance: Strong, sweet musk
Average Size: 8–15' tall × 5–10' wide
Disease Resistance: Excellent
Rebloom: Excellent
Garden Uses: Groupings, medium climber, cut flowers, own-root,
  light shade, pollinators

VINCENT GODSIFF

China, date unknown

When buying roses in a nursery, my eyes always seek out plants that are clear standouts—healthy, leafy shrubs bursting with new growth and flowers while still in their pots. 'Vincent Godsiff' is one such rose: a specimen caught my eye from the back of a nursery, radiating vigor and brimming with flowers as if posing for the cover of a catalogue.

This was in August in South Florida, by the way. Temperatures were in the high 90s, and the humidity felt like trying to breathe through a steaming washcloth. All the other potted roses nearby looked sad and defeated while 'Vincent Godsiff' stood regally, like a prince. Its garden performance over the years has been similarly unwavering.

Another of the "Bermuda Mystery" roses, 'Vincent Godsiff' resembles a China rose with long, pointed leaflets and twiggy branches sprinkled with recurved thorns. Upright, branched sprays of tapered buds open up into 2", semidouble, open-cupped blooms that start off vivid pink but darken to red by their second day. Each flower's center is highlighted with a mass of yellow stamens. Their sweet pea fragrance is refreshing and soft.

A large part of 'Vincent Godsiff's appeal lies in its wonderful versatility: the flowers have a country-casual charm, but the shrub itself is upright and formal looking. This makes for a rose equally at home in a mixed cottage garden, or the grand courtyard of a Mediterranean-style mansion in Miami or Naples.

Hybridizer: Unknown
Culture: Easy
Availability: Moderate
Fragrance: Sweet pea-ish
Average Size: 4–6' tall × 3–4' wide
Disease Resistance: Good
Rebloom: Excellent
Garden Uses: Flowerbeds, cut flowers, groupings, containers, hedge, own-root, pollinators

VIOLET'S PRIDE

Floribunda, 2017

Good lavender roses are hard to come by, and only three made my list of the best 100 roses for South Florida. 'Violet's Pride' is the least purple of the three included here, which is a bit disappointing, as any variety whose name includes a color should really embody the name. Call me tough, but I demand a lot of my roses.

That's not to say that 'Violet's Pride' isn't a great rose. The fragrance is a big plus, as the other two lavenders ('Poseidon' and 'Love Song') are only moderately scented at best. Not so with 'Violet's Pride': the full, rounded blooms emit a powerful, spicy old-rose aroma that is especially potent on warm days (most of the year for us here). The soft mauve outer petals deepen to smoky magenta in their centers, creating a lovely two-tone effect in the garden. It's a beautifully delicate coloration but not really lavender, much less "violet."

'Violet's Pride' forms a stout, rounded shrub to around 4' tall and wide, densely clad in rich green, wavy-textured leaves. Mature plants produce endless flower flushes—another strong selling point.

This rose was named for the popular *Downton Abbey* character portrayed by actress Maggie Smith. Violet Crawley, Dowager Countess of Grantham, was the imposing family matriarch of the show, frequently portrayed wearing period dresses in her namesake color.

Hybridizer: Christian Bédard
Culture: Easy
Availability: Wide
Fragrance: Intense, spicy old rose
Average Size: 4–5' tall × 4–5' wide
Disease Resistance: Good
Rebloom: Good
Garden Uses: Flowerbeds, cut flowers, groupings, hedge

WEEPING CHINA DOLL

Polyantha, 1977

Like many northern transplants in South Florida, I frequently yearn for the spring-blooming "cold climate" shrubs I grew up with. Things like weigela, forsythia, pearlbush, beautybush, and other temperate-zone shrubs have a certain iconic magic to their form: arching branches completely covered with small but brilliant flowers every spring before leaves appear. Few tropical shrubs really replicate this floral effect.

Fortunately, that's where 'Weeping China Doll' comes in. This cultivar forms a large, lofty mass of gracefully cascading, mostly thornless canes. Stems are densely lined with small, bright green leaves, typically with just three leaflets, but the foliage is frequently hidden by an avalanche of blousy, fluffy, deep pink blossoms. Individual petals are spoon shaped and curl inward, and each bloom is held on a wispy little stalk that bends under the weight of the petals, further exaggerating the weeping effect of the plant.

I can't say enough good things about 'Weeping China Doll'. Besides looking like something transported right out of springtime in New England, this rose is easy to grow and needs little fussing once established.

This variety's landscape uses are endless. Try it as a freestanding specimen, a flowering hedge, in groupings, or as a climber along a fence. I especially love 'Weeping China Doll' used as a backdrop for blush-pink roses—'Francis Meilland' or 'Puerto Rico'—to create an exciting juxtaposition of colors and textures.

Hybridizer: Robert Hardman Melville
Culture: Easy
Availability: Wide
Fragrance: Light
Average Size: 7–9' tall × 7–9' wide
Disease Resistance: Good
Rebloom: Excellent
Garden Uses: Groupings, specimen, hedge, medium climber

WINDERMERE

Shrub (David Austin), 2005

I originally planted four 'Windermere' in a prominent spot in our Oakland Park garden, where they proceeded to do nothing for the next six months—which made me worry that this variety was ill suited to South Florida. Thankfully, I waited a little longer; around the seven-month mark, I finally saw plump new basal canes and top growth forming on each. Whew!

'Windermere' is now a personal favorite, easily one of the most heavy-flowering Austins in our climate. Clusters of plump, peachy-apricot buds with stubby sepals gently open up into lovely, incurved, old-fashioned blooms of creamy ivory with a warm buttermilk glow in their centers. Cool weather blooms are phenomenally big and double, with petals arranged in perfect symmetry like a vortex. They have a delicious citrus and myrrh fragrance.

'Windermere' is also one of the handsomest Austins from a shrub point of view, forming an attractive mass of ascending canes well clothed in dark green leaves. Each leaf is attractively angled along the stem, with the terminal leaflet tipping down like a fashion model pointing a stiletto. My plants thrived on the east side of a sweet almond hedge where they received full morning sun and then were shaded from about 2:00 p.m. onward, so 'Windermere' is also a good candidate for partial shade conditions.

The name commemorates Windermere Lake, the largest natural lake in England, which is close to the David Austin nursery.

Hybridizer: David Austin
Culture: Easy
Availability: Moderate
Fragrance: Medium fruit/myrrh blend
Average Size: 5–6' tall × 4–5' wide
Disease Resistance: Good
Rebloom: Excellent
Garden Uses: Flowerbeds, cut flowers, groupings, partial shade

XANDER

Shrub, 2018

'Xander' is a pure delight—literally, as the purity of these glistening white petals is unblemished by any other hue. Flowers, always in fluffy sprays, are saucer-shaped single blossoms composed of broad, silky petals with wavy margins and a large mass of yellow and green stamens. Fully open blossoms resemble Japanese anemones in their airy gracefulness.

This cultivar's willowy canes form a billowing shrub much wider than tall. Stems are armed with small, pointed prickles all along their length. New growth is a handsome sepia color, maturing to glossy medium green, oblong leaflets with attractive serrations along their margins. 'Xander' is also a very healthy rose that doesn't need spraying to stay leafy.

'Xander' performs acceptably well as an own-root plant in South Florida. Try to get plants grafted on 'Fortuniana' if you can, however—they will grow faster and be even more floriferous.

Like most single roses, 'Xander' is highly attractive to pollinators, and the petals close up at night. Attractive, bright orange hips will form if you don't deadhead spent blooms. 'Xander's biggest drawback is its limited availability; as of this publication, only one retailer offers it for sale. If you do find 'Xander', however, get at least four or five plants—this rose is absolutely spectacular en masse.

Hybridizer: Allen Whitcomb
Culture: Easy
Availability: Limited
Fragrance: Light to none
Average Size: 3–4' × 5' wide
Disease Resistance: Good
Rebloom: Excellent
Garden Uses: Flowerbeds, cut flowers, groupings, containers, own-root, pollinators

YUKI'S DREAM

China, 2001

'Yuki's Dream' was discovered by Yuki Mikanagi while she was traveling with a group of rose aficionados in the Sichuan region of China. As per Yuki's account, she took a cutting of a beautiful, unknown rose she encountered there and rooted it in her garden back in Japan. The cutting quickly grew into a well-mannered small climber that bloomed throughout the growing season.

The two-tone flowers of 'Yuki's Dream' are carried in clusters of six or more. Small, conical buds of deep fuchsia quickly open up into semidouble blooms of pure white shaded with watermelon pink on their outer third. A mass of white and gold stamens anchors each blossom's center like a bullseye. As with many China roses, 'Yuki's Dream' is phototropic: strong sunlight will cause the pink tones to deepen and spread.

This is another rose you'll love as much for the foliage as for the flowers. 'Yuki's Dream' is cloaked in healthy, long, pointed leaflets of dark gray green with a noticeably silver flipside and handsomely serrated margins. Blackspot need not be a concern with this variety.

One word of caution: 'Yuki's Dream' has floppy canes lined with viciously sharp thorns, so careful placement is a must. I used two 'Yuki's Dream' in matching obelisks in a pink-and-purple themed garden where they flanked an 8' wide grass pathway—enough walking space to admire the blossoms without getting snagged by the painful prickles.

Discoverer: Yuki Mikanagi
Culture: Easy
Availability: Limited
Fragrance: Light
Average Size: 6–8' tall × 4' wide
Disease Resistance: Good
Rebloom: Excellent
Garden Uses: Small climber, own-root, pollinators

ZACH NOBLES

Hybrid Tea, 2012

Along with 'Francis Meilland', 'Zach Nobles' is one of the roses that made me want to explore the hybrid teas more in South Florida. Both varieties are healthy and hardly ever out of bloom here. So long as you get a 'Fortuniana'-grafted plant, this rose more than justifies its garden space.

'Zach Nobles' is a color sport of the popular red hybrid tea 'Let Freedom Ring'. Neither of these roses is fragrant, but 'Zach Nobles' has such a unique color that the scentlessness can be forgiven. Although officially listed as orange red, in South Florida the petals can range from dark coral pink to an almost smoky orange brown with lavender highlights, depending on the time of year and the intensity of the sun. Regardless of hue, these blooms are always large and beautifully crafted, emerging from equally handsome buds with ornate sepals and carried tall and proud on long stems.

As with 'Let Freedom Ring', 'Zach Nobles' (occasionally misspelled as 'Noble') forms an upright shrub cloaked in large, glossy, dark green leaves that make a handsome backdrop for the blooms. Strong disease resistance and prolific bloom make 'Zach Nobles' good for beginners—particularly those looking for an unusually colored flower to round out their garden palette.

Hybridizer: Satish M. Prabhu
Culture: Easy
Availability: Wide
Fragrance: Light to none
Average Size: 5–6' tall × 4' wide
Disease Resistance: Excellent
Rebloom: Good
Garden Uses: Flowerbeds, cut flowers, groupings

Acknowledgments

An unexpected consequence of writing my first book was the realization of how much kindness still exists in our world—for, without the generous aid and encouragement of countless friends, family members, and colleagues, *100 Roses for the South Florida Garden* might have never taken off.

For their truly indispensable help, I must thank Edwing Medina, Lindsey Joerger, Dan Sweeney, Stephen Obie, Chris Nguyen, Geoff and Debbie Coolidge, Art Wade, James Mills, Kathleen Rose, Dr. Malcolm Manners, Maria Wolfe, Debbie Hughes, Mike Becker, Bill Langford, Adriane Shochet, the entire Nelson's staff, and the utterly fabulous "Rose Gator Queen" herself, Connie Vierbicky.

Thanks also to Nirav Ramteerath, for his nonstop help with my garden photography; Vava Antar Pragya, for teaching me truly incredible means of organic gardening; Julia Howard, for encouraging my love of flowers from my earliest years; and my wonderful parents, Salvatore and Theresa Mary Lazzari, for their unconditional love and support with every project I've ever explored.

Special gratitude goes out to my editor, Stephanye Hunter, for having faith in a first-time author, and to Roberto Rovira and Justin Hancock, for their professional advice in launching this project. I am also deeply indebted to the man who inspired this book, Mr. Clair Martin, whose own books were a beacon of hope and inspiration to a shy teenage gardener in the mid-1990s.

Additional Resources

LOCAL NURSERIES—SOUTHEAST FLORIDA

Cool Roses*
(561) 313-0077
https://www.coolroses.com
Offers a huge selection of 'Fortuniana'-grafted modern roses and own-root old roses. Open by appointment only.

* The Cool Roses nursery was transitioning to a new location as this book was being published. Please check their website for the latest updates on their new address.

NuTurf Garden Center
2801 N. Dixie Highway
Pompano Beach, FL 33064
(954) 942-8409
https://www.nuturfpompano.com
Offers a good selection of 'Fortuniana'-grafted modern roses and occasionally some own-root old roses.

Jesse Durko's Nursery
5151 SW 70th Avenue
Davie, FL 33314
(954) 873-4563
http://www.jessedurko.com
Offers a modest selection of own-root old roses.

Living Color Garden Center
3691 Griffin Road
Fort Lauderdale, FL 33312
(954) 985-8787
https://livingcolorgardencenter.net
Offers a good selection of 'Fortuniana'-grafted modern roses.

Galloway Farm Nursery
7790 SW 87th Avenue
Miami, FL 33173
(305) 274-7472
https://www.gallowayfarm.com
Offers a good selection of 'Fortuniana'-grafted modern roses.

LOCAL NURSERIES—SOUTHWEST FLORIDA

Hardin's Nursery
6011 S. Dale Mabry Highway
Tampa, FL 33611
(813) 839-6151
https://www.facebook.com/hardinsnursery
Offers a huge selection of 'Fortuniana'-grafted modern roses.

Troy's Tropics
5212 Proctor Road
Sarasota, FL 34233
(941) 923-3756
https://www.troystropics.com
Offers a good selection of 'Fortuniana'-grafted modern roses.

Your Farm and Garden
735 S. Beneva Road
Sarasota, FL 34232
(941) 366-4954
https://www.yourfarmandgarden.com
Offers a good selection of 'Fortuniana'-grafted modern roses.

Driftwood Garden Center
5051 Tamiami Trail N.
Naples, FL 34103
(239) 261-0328
https://www.driftwoodgardencenter.com
Offers a modest selection of 'Fortuniana'-grafted modern roses.

Scott's Landscape Nursery
5870 Bayshore Road
North Fort Myers, FL 33917
(239) 599-4071
https://scottslandscapenursery.com
Offers a small selection of 'Fortuniana'-grafted modern roses.

ONLINE NURSERIES

K&M Roses
1260 Chicora River Road
Buckatunna, MS 39322
(601) 648-2908
https://www.kandmroses.com
Offers a huge selection of 'Fortuniana'-grafted modern roses and own-root old roses.

Rose Petals Nursery
16918 SW 15th Avenue
Newberry, FL 32669
(352) 215-6399
https://www.rosepetalsnursery.com
Offers a huge selection of own-root old roses and own-root modern roses.

The Antique Rose Emporium
9300 Lueckemeyer Road
Brenham, TX 77833
(800) 441-0002
https://www.antiqueroseemporium.com
Offers a huge selection of own-root old roses and own-root modern roses.

Rogue Valley Roses
2368 Terri Drive
Medford, OR 97504
(541) 535-1307
https://roguevalleyroses.com
Offers a huge selection of own-root old roses and own-root modern roses.

Heirloom Roses
24062 Riverside Drive NE
St. Paul, OR 97137
(800) 820-0465
https://www.heirloomroses.com
Offers a huge selection of own-root old roses and own-root modern roses.

PUBLIC ROSE GARDENS

Mounts Botanical Garden
531 N. Military Trail
West Palm Beach, FL 33415
(561) 233-1757
https://www.mounts.org
A 14-acre botanical garden featuring various roses planted alongside over 6,000 other species of tropical and subtropical plants.

Vizcaya Museum and Gardens
3251 S. Miami Avenue
Miami, FL 33129
(305) 250-9133
https://vizcaya.org
A 43-acre historical estate featuring a large rose garden designed in an elaborate Italian Renaissance style.

Edison and Ford Winter Estates
2350 McGregor Boulevard
Fort Myers, FL 33901
(239) 334-7419

https://www.edisonfordwinterestates.org
A 20-acre historical estate featuring several rose garden areas along with over 1,000 additional species of tropical and subtropical plants.

NONPROFIT ORGANIZATIONS

Greater Palm Beach Rose Society
https://gpbrs.org
Serves Palm Beach and Martin counties.

Tropical Rose Society of Greater Miami
https://www.tropicalrose.org
Serves Miami-Dade and Broward counties.

Bradenton-Sarasota Rose Society
https://www.b-srs.org
Serves Manatee and Sarasota counties.

American Rose Society
https://www.rose.org
National rose society of the United States.

Deep South District
https://deepsouthdistrict.org/
Represents rose societies throughout Florida, Georgia, and Alabama.

American Rose Trials for Sustainability
https://www.americanrosetrialsforsustainability.org
National organization for identifying the most sustainable, low-maintenance, eco-friendly roses for the United States.

FOR FURTHER READING

Austin, David. *The English Roses: Classic Favorites & New Selections*. 3rd ed. New York: Firefly Books, 2017.
Druitt, Liz. *The Organic Rose Garden*. Lanham, MD: Taylor Trade, 1996.
Edinger, Philip. *Sunset Roses*. Menlo Park: Sunset, 1990.

Grant, Greg, and William C. Welch. *The Rose Rustlers*. College Station: Texas A&M University Press, 2017.

HelpMeFind (database). "Help Me Find: Roses, Clematis and Peonies." Last modified October 2021. http://www.helpmefind.com/roses/.

Martin, Clair G. *100 English Roses for the American Garden*. New York: Workman, 1997.

———. *100 Old Roses for the American Garden*. New York: Workman, 1999.

Nelson, Mark. *Nelson's Guide to Florida Roses*. Orlando: Waterview Press, 2003.

Shoup, G. Michael. *Roses in the Southern Garden*. Brenham, TX: Antique Rose Emporium, 2000.

Welch, William C. *Antique Roses for the South*. Lanham, MD: Taylor Trade, 2004.

Index

Page numbers in *italics* refer to illustrations. Page numbers in *italics* followed by the letter *t* indicate tables.

VICTOR LAZZARI is a landscape designer, garden writer, and horticulturist originally from the hilly farm country of Maryland, where a deep love of all things green and growing first took hold of him as a small child. He holds a BA in Landscape Design (University of Maryland), an MA in Landscape Architecture (Florida International University), and a Masters Certificate in Agroecology (also FIU).

A Florida resident since 2007, Victor's passion has always been English-inspired flower gardens as well as any garden that incorporates roses. He has been growing and evaluating roses for the past 25 years and frequently includes them in landscape design work for clients.

Victor currently resides in Cape Coral, Florida, with his partner, Brian, and their two kids: Teddy, a saucy tuxedo cat, and Tyson, a sycophantic black lab mix with an unhealthy fixation on tennis balls.

100 Roses for the South Florida Garden is Victor's first book.